MANAGING
CONVERSATIONS WITH
HOSTILE ADULTS

MANAGING
CONVERSATIONS WITH HOSTILE ADULTS

Strategies for Teachers

GEORGIA J. KOSMOSKI   DENNIS R. POLLACK

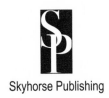

Skyhorse Publishing

Skyhorse Publishing books may be purchased in bulk at special discounts for sales promotion, corporate gifts, fund-raising, or educational purposes. Special editions can also be created to specifications. For details, contact the Special Sales Department, Skyhorse Publishing, 307 West 36th Street, 11th Floor, New York, NY 10018 or info@skyhorsepublishing.com.

Skyhorse® and Skyhorse Publishing® are registered trademarks of Skyhorse Publishing, Inc.®, a Delaware corporation.

Visit our website at www.skyhorsepublishing.com.

10 9 8 7 6 5 4 3 2 1

Library of Congress Cataloging-in-Publication Data is available on file.

Cover design by Michael Dubowe

Print ISBN: 978-1-62914-745-1
Ebook ISBN: 978-1-63220-041-9

Printed in the United States of America

Contents

Contents

Preface

Many school administrators are finding that hostile conversations with adults in school settings are becoming more commonplace and intense. These conversations range from annoying situations in the faculty lounge, where peers or subordinates whine and gripe, to incidents in which parents or community members loudly harangue us at public meetings, to encounters with out-of-control individuals under the influence of drugs or alcohol. Tragedies, such as the series of fatal shootings in a half dozen schools, have made us mindful of our precarious position. But what actions should we take to reduce the risk, safeguard the schools, and effectively communicate with those who are hostile to us? Consider the following vignette.

While enjoying coffee with my friend Dave, superintendent of a midsized suburban school district, I listened as he related an unnerving incident that had happened to him a few days earlier. Dave explained that as he was leaving the central office building, an agitated stranger confronted him. A large red-faced man blocked the path to his car in the deserted parking lot and began screaming about the school district's plan to institute a uniform dress policy for students. Dave admitted that with all the violent school-related acts reported in the news lately, his first reaction was fear.

As he recounted the story, however, it became evident that no serious consequences came from the incident. He handled the encounter well. He calmed the man down, defused the situation, and arranged a later meeting where he could control the setting and circumstances.

Dave's story sparked my curiosity. I asked him what techniques he used to defuse this potentially dangerous scenario. After a few thoughtful seconds, he admitted that he really wasn't sure. He said that he had simply reacted by doing what seemed appropriate.

Dave is not the exception to the rule. Successful school administrators ought to have excellent verbal and interpersonal skills. Many do. However, like Dave, few administrators are actually aware of the strategies they use during stressful conversations.

We all operate by a personal set of rules to cope with difficult situations. Also, we create strategies to implement our rules. If, like Dave, we encounter an individual who has antagonistic rules that are alien to us, we must devise a new set of proven strategies to engage them and defuse the situation.

If school administrators could identify and apply the strategies that are proven successful when dealing with hostile adults in schools, they would have additional tools to be effective leaders. Rather than just reacting to potentially dangerous confrontations, administrators could become proactive.

These considerations, along with Dave's experience, became the catalyst for a study spanning eight years. During this research study, we surveyed and interviewed in depth over 250 actively practicing school administrators. The study identified the most stressful verbal confrontations school administrators face with adults in our schools, and the proven strategies that help us effectively communicate and defuse those situations.

This book is based on the information gained from the aforementioned study. The first 11 chapters address the most stressful encounters. The vignettes told in each chapter are true stories shared with us by the study participants. The names, places, and times were changed to maintain confidentiality. After reading the opening vignette you, the reader, are encouraged to ask several self-reflective questions. Would I have managed this situation similarly or differently? How would I have acted? Why would I behave this way? How well did the administrator manage the encounter? What skills can I learn and apply from this example?

As you read the other sections, you might have your analysis affirmed, or you might learn new solutions that you have never before utilized, or the chapter analysis might serve as a trigger for your mind to create yet a better strategy.

The vignettes serve as a starting point, and then each of the vignettes is rated for the level of stress it engenders. Although varying encounters elicit different stress levels in individuals, the rating given to each story is an average for the study participants.

Each chapter analyzes the motives and actions of the hostile adult and the effectiveness of the school administrator in managing the situation. The psychological and administrative viewpoints are presented. Strategies and suggestions for application to additional circumstances are highlighted.

The first 11 "story" chapters are ordered in a manner to aid in comprehension and application. There are eight sections in each. Each section has a specific purpose to help you in your learning journey. They are:

1. The Story—a true story shared by a colleague.

2. How Taxing Are Such Encounters?—the average "stress" score of 250 study participants.

3. A Psychological Perspective of This Situation—an analysis of the actions and behaviors of the hostile individual.

4. A Practitioner's View—an analysis of the performance of the involved administrator from an educational adminis-tration framework.

5. A Clinical View—an analysis of the performance of the involved administrator from a psychology framework.

6. Additional Suggestions—a collection of additional recom-mended strategies that would be useful in situations of this nature. These strategies are not all-inclusive but are those most often suggested by the study group.

7. In What Other Cases Do the Learned Techniques Apply?—a collection of situations where the discussed strategies would be most helpful. Again, these are not all-inclusive.

8. Summary—an encapsulation of the recommended strate-gies or best practices.

At the end of each chapter, you will find a list of Suggested Readings, a list of reading material that is germane to the topic discussed. Chapter 12 is separate and unique from the previous 11 chapters. It identifies and explains the 15 most effective strate-gies used in hostile conversations. These strategies provide us with a collection of skills useful in our profession. The book concludes with Resource A, the Kosmoski/Pollack School Administrators'

Code of Ethics, which provides the practitioner with a foundation on which to operate successfully.

Skill in communicating is essential in our profession. The wisdom of our colleagues can help us deal successfully with conversations with hostile adults. If we can apply these identified strategies during hostile conversations, we will become more effective educational leaders in today's schools.

ACKNOWLEDGMENTS

We gratefully acknowledge the contributions of the following reviewers:

John W. Cook
Assistant Principal
Chicago, Illinois

Robert Denham
Interim Dean
School of Education
University of Redlands
Redlands, California

Virginia Drouin
Principal
Alfred Elementary School
Alfred, Maine

Sondra Estep
Director, Adventures of the
    American Mind
Governors State University
University Park, Illinois

Bill Grobe
Junior Division Teacher
Mother Teresa Catholic School
Waterloo Catholic District
    School Board
Cambridge, Ontario

Glenna Howell
Professor of Education
Governors State University
University Park, Illinois

Harry Hufty
Principal
School District 57
Prince George, British
    Columbia

Jeff Jones
Assistant Principal
Calgary Board of
    Education
Calgary, Alberta

Beatrice Lingenfelter
Assistant Professor
Benerd School of Education
University of the Pacific
Stockton, California

Bert Lundgren
High School English Chair
    (Retired)
Big Horn, Wyoming

E. Von Mansfield
Principal
Homewood Flossmoor
    High School
Flossmoor, Illinois

Phil McCullum
Assistant Director
Administrator Licensure
    Program
University of Oregon
Eugene, Oregon

Michele Merkle
Principal
York Suburban High School
York, Pennsylvania

Gretchen Ricker
Associate Director
Texas Elementary Principals
    and Supervisors
Austin, Texas

Lou Rollenhagen
Principal
Palisade High School
Palisade, Colorado

Carol Spencer
Founder/Director
Best Practice Designs
Addison, Vermont

Dana Trevethan
Principal
Turlock High School
Turlock, California

Patti Vickery
Principal
Woodsboro Junior
    High School
Woodsboro, Texas

In addition, we would like to express our gratitude to the following for their contributions: Kim Gordon, Joliet, IL; Claudia Harris, Chicago, IL; Lynn Merrick, Lockport, IL; Carey Radde, Bolingbrook, IL; Mary Shaffer, Manteno, IL; Nora Skentzos, Lockport, IL; and Rita Stasi, Downers Grove, IL.

About the Authors

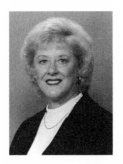 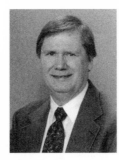 Together, **Kosmoski** and **Pollack** are the coauthors of the book *Managing Conversations With Hostile Adults: Strategies for Teachers* (2001), which is the parallel book for teachers to this publication. Today, these authors are members of the Corwin Speakers Bureau and present workshops and seminars across the country for school districts and educational organizations on topics such as handling hostile conversations, confronting student suicide, and finding a job in school administration.

CHAPTER ONE

Defusing the Angry Screamer

THE STORY: Rant and Rave

THE PLACE: An Impoverished City Junior High School

J ohn Cooke is the veteran junior high school vice principal of discipline for 900 adolescents. John has had plenty of practice calming down young people. He is no stranger to agitated, volatile, and hostile individuals. Silent pouting, crying, and irrational screaming are behaviors he encounters on a regular basis.

John Cooke finished straightening his desktop. He looked at his daily planner for tomorrow's schedule. Yes, Thursday looked like an average day. John glanced at his watch; it was already 4:15 p.m. Where did the day go? It was too late to drop off his discipline reports. He would have to do that on his way to school the next morning.

As he stuffed the reports and several other files into his brief-case, he heard a loud voice coming from the outer office. John sighed and slipped on his sport coat as he headed for the connecting door. Just one more thing to take care of before heading out.

Opening the door, John was greeted by the sight of a short, burly, middle-aged man leaning over the counter. The visitor was sweating profusely, slamming his hand repeatedly against the countertop, and yelling at Mrs. Williams, the office receptionist. His face was livid with anger and his jugular vein coursed with blood. Mrs. Williams was the only person left in the office and seemed very relieved to see John Cooke enter. John nodded at her and said in a level tone, "Thank you, Mrs. Williams. That will be all." Mrs. Williams immediately backed away, averted her eyes, and returned to her desk.

Before John could reach the counter or introduce himself, the man rounded on him. "Who the hell are you? I want some answers and I want them now."

In direct contrast to the man's booming, shrill, and breathless voice, John spoke slowly and kept his voice low and calm. He stated, "I'm John Cooke, the vice principal here. May I have your name, sir?"

Ignoring John's remarks, the man thrust his hand into his pants pocket and produced a half-sheet of crumpled yellow paper. John recognized the paper as a Discipline Action Report form that is sent home to parents. The man peered at the paper and then at John. "Yeah, you're the idiot I'm looking for. Just what the f___ is this?" With that, he threw the slip at John's face. Before John could grab it, the paper fluttered to the floor on his side of the counter. Cautiously, John bent down and retrieved the paper. He laid it on the counter, smoothed it out, read it, and used the opportunity to calm himself. While John perused the slip, the outraged parent continued to rant and rave. The man sputtered something about "getting him" for being a troublemaker. This angry man did not seem to need to stop to breathe.

Recalling the student's last name on the action sheet, John Cooke took a chance and cut in. He said, "Mr. Crass?" But the man did not respond to the use of the surname, Crass. John therefore concluded that he had correctly guessed the man's last name and continued, "It sounds like you have some concerns regarding this Saturday's in-school suspension for your daughter, Carrie."

"You're damn right! What the hell do you think you're doing here? You're not going to get away with this. We have other plans for Saturday and if I have to, I'll get a lawyer to stop this Saturday prison," screamed Mr. Crass.

John studied the man more closely. His fists were clenched, his upper torso rigid, and his voice very loud and shaky. Mr. Crass seemed to be struggling to keep verbal and physical control of himself. John concluded that what he was witnessing was an adult temper tantrum.

John Cooke vowed that he would not let Mr. Crass's tirade and manner intimidate or upset him. While Crass sputtered, John made eye contact, nodded, and regularly interjected short, active listening phrases such as "I hear you are upset with me," "What did I do to upset you?" and "I see you are very angry and upset."

After about a minute, John Cooke attempted to direct the conversation to the points he needed to make. He proceeded, "Mr. Crass, I can see that this matter is very important to you. I'm glad you are concerned about Carrie. I care about her too. We do need to talk about the situation and resolve this issue. But right now we are both pretty upset and it's hard to think clearly. We really have a lot to discuss. I understand that we have to clear this up before Saturday. I really want to take our time and come to a fair understanding. No rushing."

Mr. Crass nodded his head and let out an affirmative grunt. John hurried on before he could be sidetracked, "Unfortunately, I'm already late for a meeting that has been scheduled for some time at the district office. Could you possibly come in tomorrow or Friday afternoon so we can sit down together and do what's best for Carrie?"

For the first time, Mr. Crass was silent. He appeared to think before speaking. When Crass spoke again, his voice was more controlled and level. He responded gruffly, "Well, I guess I might be able to get here about the same time tomorrow. You know, some of us do work."

John put on a big grin and replied, "That's great! I'll clear my schedule so we have all the time we need to resolve your concerns. Do you know your way back to where you parked?" Mr. Crass nodded and moved toward the office door. John waved and said goodbye, as Mr. Crass gently closed the office door behind him.

Mrs. Williams smiled and shook her head as she collected her purse and jacket. She turned to John and said, "Thanks, Mr. Cooke. You were great. That's another R&R on ice."

John was puzzled. "Rest and relaxation on ice?" he asked. "No," said Mrs. Williams as she turned the hall doorknob, "A ranter and raver in the cooler. See you in the morning."

HOW TAXING ARE SUCH ENCOUNTERS?

All of the 250 school administrators surveyed reported that they had been confronted by a person who ranted and raved. Not one was immune to this type of verbal attack. The great majority who felt they had handled the situation successfully had used a calm and rational approach. Most school administrators who felt that they had had an unsuccessful experience admitted that they had engaged in a yelling contest. They acknowledged that they had screamed as much as the other party involved.

When asked how stressful this type of situation is to them, the administrators responded this was a **5–most stressful.**

5–most stressful	4–more stressful	3– stressful	2–little stress	1–no stress

A PSYCHOLOGICAL PERSPECTIVE OF THIS SITUATION: WHAT DO WE KNOW ABOUT PEOPLE WHO YELL TO GET THEIR WAY?

Anger is about power. The very angry individual who is acting inappropriately does not feel that his or her opinions or feelings are being recognized, adequately considered, given any weight, or accepted. Mr. Crass was willing to force his point of view on another person. How far he was willing to go was indicated by his inappropriate behavior. He had burst into the main office, yelled at the secretary, yelled at the assistant principal, thrown a note onto the floor in an attempt to humiliate the administrator, and used very inappropriate language in a school setting. The amount of socially inappropriate behavior is a good measure of the anger of the individual. It is also a good measure of the actual threat to school safety.

Mr. Cooke quickly attempted to engage Mr. Crass with a friendly greeting. He was not only rebuffed, but Mr. Crass tried to escalate the meeting into a confrontation when he threw the form in Mr. Cooke's face. This was an attempt to elicit anger from Mr. Cooke, so that the confrontation could be taken further—it was, in effect, a challenge to a duel. If dueling were still in vogue, Mr. Cooke might have been looking for a second. Fortunately, that aspect of the age of chivalry is dead. Instead of responding to the dueling challenge, Mr. Cooke acted like a gentleman and picked up the paper. By this act, he began to disarm his adversary. It is true that by picking up the paper, he put himself in a vulnerable position, but it was this act that caught Mr. Crass by surprise.

When John calmly placed the piece of paper on the counter, he indicated that, unlike Mr. Crass, he was going to act in a socially appropriate manner. John's controlled behavior subtly suggested to Crass that the piece of paper was important to both of them. He allowed Crass to continue to rant and rave because he was not going to respond to an attempt at personal contact until Crass had said what was on his mind. John understood that he had an issue and the right to express it. That the forum was wrong was not important, because Crass was not going to listen to issues of social convention. Mr. Crass clearly wanted to express his anger and contempt to someone and John recognized that he was going to be that someone. It was not a pleasant administrative task, but it was one of the roles for which he had been hired.

John approached Mr. Crass gently, rather than retorting in anger. He not only could hear Crass's anger, but also could see it. This was someone who was willing to go beyond the bounds of acceptable behavior. John posited that Mr. Crass would not really go beyond yelling, so he decided to assuage Mr. Crass's anger by accepting it.

People like Mr. Crass frequently do not recognize the intensity of their emotions, and need others to identify it. Once they recognize it in themselves, they may decide that it is not the way they want or intend to act. By speaking softly and using such phrases as "I hear you" and "I see you are very angry and upset," John told Mr. Crass that he was angry. Why? For two reasons: first, to let Mr. Crass know that he understood and recognized that he was upset; second, and most important, to identify to Mr. Crass how angry he was.

When John said that he recognized how important this confrontation was to Mr. Crass, he co-opted his issue. He made it his issue as well. This was disarming, and Mr. Crass lost his reason to be angry. By acknowledging the anger and co-opting the issue, John was able to begin negotiations to reconcile the difference between Mr. Crass and himself.

HOW WELL DID THE VICE PRINCIPAL HANDLE THE RANTING PARENT?

A Practitioner's View

John Cooke's behavior during this incident is commendable. Throughout the entire event, John remained calm, maintained his wits, and successfully defused the situation. Vice Principal Cooke did an excellent job of regulating his voice: He controlled both his volume and speed. A low, slow, and calm delivery is nonthreatening. It has a soothing effect on the listener.

John was very careful in choosing his words. His remarks showed concern and professionalism. He neither threatened nor showed signs of intimidation. Regardless of Mr. Crass's ravings, John established the most needed elements for closure. He was able to identify with Mr. Crass and address his grievance. John shifted the emphasis during the exchange from *I'll* get the authority figure to *we'll* work together to help our daughter/student. John's creative use of the phrases " . . . we are both upset right now . . ." and " . . . we can sit down together and do what's best for Carrie," was superb. These comments accomplished two things. John made Mr. Crass an ally in the common purpose of helping a child, and he arranged for a problem-solving meeting at a time when Mr. Crass would most probably be calmed down. Mr. Cooke's words and delivery gave him more control of the situation.

John Cooke was able to depersonalize the situation. By recognizing that he was witnessing an adult temper tantrum, he was better able to control his own feelings and behavior. This gave him an enormous advantage during the confrontation.

Finally, whether by accident or design, John did the prudent thing by keeping the counter between Mr. Crass and himself during the tirade. Although it is rare for shouters to resort to physical violence, it is always a genuine possibility. Personal safety during any screaming encounter must be a priority.

A Clinical View

John handled this situation with the equanimity and aplomb to which we all aspire. For many of us, our major failing is that when someone becomes angry with us, we want to respond in self-defense. Sometimes this manifests itself as anger. To illustrate, suppose you are driving down the freeway and someone cuts you off. You respond with a few choice words and angry gestures. Is the other person going to remain civil? Most likely he, too, is going to respond angrily. You threw down the gauntlet when you vocalized and physically expressed your anger. The other driver is simply picking up the gauntlet. You now get to have a chance at dueling cars, a.k.a. road rage. You are advised to take John's approach and not respond. Life is too short and need not end on the freeway or in the school office because you are tempted to engage in a duel of unbridled emotions.

ADDITIONAL SUGGESTIONS: WHAT ELSE COULD AND SHOULD YOU DO IN SIMILAR SITUATIONS?

1. John Cooke did a good job of remaining calm throughout this entire incident. Sometimes this is not easily accomplished. How does one calm oneself? Several proven tactics will help you attain this goal. Take a deep breath before speaking. This gives you a few seconds to gather yourself and provides at least a small measure of personal control. Then, throughout the encounter, focus on your breathing. Are you taking short, shallow breaths or barely taking any breaths at all? Force yourself to breathe slowly and deeply. This provides a mechanism for both physical and emotional control, which, in turn, results in an increased level of calmness. Another method to help you remain calm is to create emotional distance for yourself (Felder, 1994). It is very useful to repeat silently such statements as "His anger has really nothing to do with me," "I'm watching an adult temper tantrum," and "This is not personal." Jeffrey Kottler (1997) refers to emotional distancing as detachment. He explains that this practice allows you to step back and disengage from the personal aspects of a conflict so you can effectively respond without being distracted by feelings or anger. Detachment allows you to avoid "getting sucked into the vortex of his (the yeller's) anger" (p. 26).

2. Prepare appropriate and effective retorts before you encounter the next screamer. Individuals deal more effectively

with familiar situations. Successful practitioners stated that they developed a personal collection of comebacks that they rehearsed and then used successfully. These school administrators drew from their memory banks when a situation called for an effective line. They had practiced, and now felt more familiar in a given situation. This preparation eliminates the need to try to develop a creative response during the heat of battle. In essence, this practice is a form of self-training. Training is necessary for school personnel in this, as well as in a myriad of other communication areas (Rubin, 1998). A few useful rejoinders might include, "Hold on! I want to be able to hear you correctly, so you'll have to slow down a little." Or perhaps, "I won't interrupt you. Just take your time and tell me the whole thing. I will speak only when you're finished." A third possibility might be, "Go ahead. I'm listening. Why don't you start at the beginning and tell me all about it." You will notice that these examples, like the ones you will soon develop, are positive statements rather than criticisms. They attempt to be nonthreatening and nondefensive. Each places you in the position of being a facilitator who respects the other individual. Finally, they all maintain a high degree of professionalism (Felder, 1994).

3. Although this vignette does not highlight the need to be a good active listener, active listening is a most useful skill when dealing with a person who is ranting and raving. Remember to use facial and body language, posture, and gestures that convey your genuine interest and concern. Small things such as eye contact, nodding, and leaning in will have a large impact on the final outcome.

4. Good timing is central to positive communication with the yeller. Sometimes the person is in such a rage that it is impossible for him or her to calm down enough to have a productive exchange of ideas. In this scenario, the wise administrator knows discussion is best delayed until the person has his or her anger under control—until he or she has cooled off. The wait time, however, should not last so long as to become fuel for additional anger. Usually, postponing a meeting for 24 hours is a good rule of thumb.

5. Finally, taking safety precautions when you are verbally attacked by a yeller is essential. Prevention is always preferable to

treatment (Phillips, 1997; Queen, 2004). If at all possible, make sure you have an available avenue of retreat. Use self-reflection or brainstorming to determine possible safety actions before a confrontation occurs.

IN WHAT OTHER CASES DO THE LEARNED TECHNIQUES APPLY?

Unfortunately, people who rant and rave come in all shapes, sizes, and ages. Both men and women are capable of yelling fits. Screamers live in all neighborhoods, belong to all cultures and ethnicities, and come from every socioeconomic group. Bosses and dependent children are equally capable of throwing a tantrum. They can lose self-control and revert to negative behavior. Therefore, practicing school administrators will inevitably find themselves confronted from time to time by angry screamers. There is no documented evidence that demonstrates that certain administrators are less susceptible than others (Lewis & Carifio, 1997).

The suggestions provided regarding Mr. Crass are effective and valid with any individual. Calmness, active listening, practice, and good timing are the keys to handling these individuals successfully (Berman, 1998; Gordon, 1998; McEwan, 2004).

SUMMARY

- Understand that screamers belong to every group of people and that you will inevitably confront them during your tenure as a school administrator.
- When faced with a person who is ranting and raving, control both your voice and your choice of words, so as to be neither threatening nor intimidating.
- Depersonalize the tirade in your own mind. The yelling is not about you.
- Determine the particulars of the events that triggered the behavior. Who's complaining and why? What are the related circumstances and concerns? What outcome is the individual seeking?

- Be cautious when dealing with an angry screamer. Such individuals can lose physical control. Take safety precautions for yourself and bystanders.
- Learn and practice techniques that will aid you in remaining calm and in personal control. Some techniques worth developing are breathing properly, distancing, and predetermining a collection of appropriate comebacks.
- Sharpen your active listening skills. Use facial expressions and body language, posture, and gestures that convey genuine interest and concern. These are great assets during these encounters.
- Remember, some confrontations are better postponed until the yeller has more control of himself or herself. Wait until the person cools off to resolve the situation.

SUGGESTED READINGS

McEwan, E. K. (2004). *How to deal with parents who are angry, afraid, or just plain crazy* (2nd ed.). Thousand Oaks, CA: Corwin.

Ramsey, R. D. (2004). *What matters most for school leaders: 25 reminders of what is really important.* Thousand Oaks, CA: Corwin.

CHAPTER TWO

Dealing With Embarrassment or Humiliation

THE STORY: Beet Red and Feeling Like the School Dunce

THE PLACE: Marvin's Cafe on Route 46 Outside of Littletown, Indiana

It was Tuesday, November 13, at 6:00 a.m. Daniel Ortega was feeling very pleased and flattered that the district superintendent had invited him to breakfast. Yesterday, Superintendent Clayton Madson had informed him that several of the leading citizens wanted to get to know him better. Madson thought that the regular Tuesday breakfast meeting at Marvin's Cafe on Route 46 was a nice, informal way to start. Clayton Madson explained that the word in town was that Dan was doing a good job as the new high school principal.

Sure! Dan knew better. This was a very important opportunity and a delicate situation. He felt excited and perhaps a little wary. This meeting could do much to either cement his position in the community or keep him a social and political outsider.

Upon entering the roadside diner, Dan spotted his superintendent sitting near the back. Two green Formica tables were pushed together, and four men in their fifties and early sixties were already sipping morning coffee. There was one empty seat next to Superintendent Madson. Taking his cue, Dan Ortega took a deep breath, waved, and plastered on his famous easy grin as he made his way to his designated chair.

As Dan shook hands all the way around, he was not surprised by the makeup of this group. In the last four months, he had heard the names of these men mentioned around school and read about them in the local paper. Besides Clayton Madson, there was Walt Jensen, real estate developer and owner of Littletown's new and only shopping mall. Dan wondered if he was connected to the Jensen Food Marts that dotted the area. Next to Jensen sat Buddy Orenberg. Dan already knew him. Buddy was president of the Littletown High School Alumni Association, as well as a full partner in the law firm of Gray, Orenberg, and Reed. Dan had heard that Orenberg had served two terms as a state representative before coming back home to run the law offices after Judge Gray retired. Orenberg apparently still had strong connections in the capitol. The other two men were Charlie Moore, president of the Lion's Club, and Frank Ellis, who was big in corn and soybeans. Just as Superintendent Madson completed the introductions, Dr. Herman McDonald, president of the school board, grabbed a chair from an empty table and squeezed in. He shook Dan's hand and praised him for having such a good start on the job. Dan smiled broadly and made a mental note to find out more about these powerful men.

The conversation around the breakfast table was both lively and convivial. These seemed to be very genuine and cordial men. Twice there had been spontaneous laughter, and on one occasion Frank Ellis laughed so hard that he choked on his coffee.

Shortly after Mary Pauline cleared the dishes away, Buddy turned to Dan and asked, "What was all the fuss about the Summers' youngest boy last Friday? What's his name? Louis?" Before Dan could get out one word, Superintendent Madson broke in.

He put his hand on Dan's shoulder and said, "Man, oh, man! Nothing gets by you, Buddy. It was a good thing I happened to be over at the high school at the time or this young man would have been in some serious sheep dip."

"Well, to come to the point, Dan was tracking down a case of alleged cheating. He had Louis Summers, Emily Summers's last child, on the carpet in his office. No hard proof, mind you. The kid did look pretty guilty, but he never admitted a thing. Dan was *soooo* dumb. He kept pressing the kid. Like that would work in Littletown."

All the men around the table looked startled and turned to peer at Dan. Some shifted and a few even snickered. Dan flushed. He felt the heat rising up his neck to his cheeks. But Clayton Madson was merciless. He threw up both hands in exasperation and continued, "Believe it or not, Dan didn't know anything about the Summers' lawsuit, and all the trouble we had with their daughter back in '99. This fool was planning on calling in the parents and suspending the kid. If I hadn't taken over, Dan could have been packing his bag and heading right back to the big city. He would have had the shortest career as school principal we've ever seen in this county."

All the men at the table burst into laughter. Dan knew he was as red as a beet. He stammered how sorry he was and something about having a lot yet to learn. Dan Ortega felt totally embarrassed. His boss had just publicly humiliated him and now was laughing at his expense with the rest of his cronies.

Dan wanted to run. He was shaking inside. He felt helpless and betrayed. Breakfast lasted another five minutes. Those minutes seemed like an eternity, and the cheerful farewells seemed insincere and hollow. Dan Ortega felt like the "Indiana school dunce."

Later, sitting in his car in the space reserved for him at the high school, he felt his fury rise. He hated what his boss had done to him. And, more important, Dan knew that he, himself, should have handled the situation better. He wasn't happy with himself. Dan vowed to formulate a plan of action before something like this ever happened to him again. Dan Ortega, school dunce, wouldn't be meekly led to the woodshed another time.

HOW TAXING ARE SUCH ENCOUNTERS?

Encountering public embarrassment, ridicule, or humiliation happens to everyone sooner or later. As one becomes more visible and influential, the possibility of such occurrences increases. School administrators must expect that they will be confronted with such situations. The question is not, therefore, what to do *if* one is publicly embarrassed but, rather, how to deal professionally with the incident when it does occur. Of the 250 administrators who shared their stories, 222 related incidents of public ridicule, humiliation, or embarrassment. The interviewed school administrators found this type of encounter a **5–most stressful.**

5–most stressful	4–more stressful	3– stressful	2–little stress	1–no stress

A PSYCHOLOGICAL PERSPECTIVE OF THIS SITUATION: WHAT DO WE KNOW ABOUT PEOPLE WHO PUBLICLY EMBARRASS OR HUMILIATE OTHERS?

Dan Ortega's situation had one obvious perpetrator and several acquiescent participants. Dr. Madson is the superintendent of schools. He is not the village idiot. He definitely had some specific purpose in mind. He was demonstrating to Dan and to the breakfast club members his absolute control. In the scenario, the breakfast club members expressed no chagrin, nor did they attempt to alleviate Dan's suffering. Either they were Madson's fellow travelers or they, themselves, had been humiliated in one of Dr. Madson's carefully directed dramas. The most generous hypothesis is that they had been overwhelmed by him and, therefore, were afraid to challenge his actions.

People such as Dr. Madson want power. Power is their goal because it usually brings money and control. In this case, control is the issue. The greater the power, the greater the control. The greater the control, the greater the pleasure derived. Dr. Madson exercised his power over Dan and used the other club members as his audience. He achieved the desired laughter at Dan's expense. In the eyes of the club, Dan will never be a threat to Madson. Clayton Madson marked his territory.

Some people use humiliation because they are insensitive to its effects. They see only the humor in the embarrassment of the victim. Where does this behavior come from? Sometimes it occurs early within one's family constellation—in childhood.

Consider your own family. Who is the butt of jokes by other family members? Usually, it is the oldest sibling who is the perpetrator of jokes at the expense of younger family members. Yet, it is the oldest who reacts to humiliation the most strongly. Unbelievably, it is common for the learning disabled child to bear the brunt of family jokes. How easy is it for the youngest to correct the oldest sibling in your family? How easy is it for the learning disabled child to correct the academically successful child? In both circumstances, the weak are at the mercy of the strong.

As adults, we tend to transfer accepted family behaviors into our social and professional lives. If we are fortunate, as we grow, our insensitive behaviors are corrected and we learn from our mistakes. However, if left unchecked, there is no reason for us to change our behaviors. Obviously, Dr. Madson was never corrected and never learned sensitivity.

He demonstrates no knowledge or skill in the newly defined area of interpersonal intelligence. Research demonstrates that had Superintendent Madson developed the necessary ability to feel and convey genuine sensitivity, his entire organization would be strengthened. People who work together in situations where positive interdependence and empathy exist exhibit higher achievement levels, self-esteem, esteem for others, motivation, task enjoyment, creativity, and thought processes (Gardner, 1994, 1995; Goleman, 1998; Goleman, Boyatzes, & McKee, 2002; Lazear, 1991). In this case, Dr. Madson has yet to learn sensitivity and Dan is at his mercy. At this time, can Dan Ortega successfully change Dr. Madson's attitudes and behavior? Certainly not!

HOW WELL DID THE NEW PRINCIPAL HANDLE THIS PUBLIC EMBARRASSMENT?

A Practitioner's View

Dan Ortega handled this situation better than one would think at first glance. Admittedly, he did not use a number of responses that probably would have successfully defused, or at least lightened, the situation. However, Dan did refrain from a host of responses that would have made the scenario even worse. There are three mistakes that he avoided and are worth exploring.

First, Dan behaved professionally when he did not retaliate with anger. He could have lashed out at his superintendent for what he viewed as a personal betrayal. He did not. Verbally lashing out at his boss in this setting would have gained nothing and instead caused additional grief for himself and the others (Lee, 1993). Yelling or chastising the assembled men for their heartless or insensitive attitudes would have served no useful purpose. Dan was wise to avoid making potential enemies.

Second, Dan Ortega might have stalked out of the diner. He did not. If Dan had run, he would have left himself with few choices: apologize, grovel, or resign. By holding his ground, he at least kept his options open. He did not put himself into an untenable position.

Finally, Dan maintained a professional demeanor when he faced the onslaught without making unnecessary and excessive excuses. Dan could have whined and/or made insincere apologies (Carlson, 1997). He might have "wimped out." Fortunately, Dan Ortega did not.

A Clinical View

This is an exceedingly complex situation. First, looking at the effect on Dan, we know that he has been taken to the proverbial woodshed. Whatever sense of control he felt he had was taken away from him. His sense of "who he was" in the community was shattered. His sense of "where he stood" with the people who hired him was destroyed. His ability to rely on his own judgment was mightily shaken. And, perhaps worst of all, he was totally unprepared for it.

We are all aware that if we want to increase a behavior, we reward it. If we want to eliminate a behavior, we either ignore it or punish it. Less well known is the way to eliminate a behavior most quickly. To do that, we punish the behavior immediately and severely (Bandura, 1977; Skinner, 1953). What is difficult about this situation for Dan is that he is torn between the sense of reward and punishment.

To illustrate this problem, consider this story. Today, I want to train my Irish wolfhound puppy to fetch the newspaper. On past occasions, the dog was trained to respond to reward. The reward was a biscuit, a pat, or both. Now, I take the dog outside, pick up the newspaper, and put it in the dog's mouth. The dog holds the paper. I say, "Fetch." I have the dog drop the newspaper in my hand and say, "Good dog." Finally, I reward him with a pat and biscuit. After many repetitions, the dog is trained to fetch the newspaper.

One day I wake up angry and hostile. I say, "Fetch" and the dog brings me the newspaper. *I respond with a sharp kick.* Will my relationship with my dog ever be the same? No! Will the dog ever be the same? No!

Will Dan ever be the same? No! In his own way, Dan expected a reward. He expected approval and acceptance. Instead of the reward of approval and acceptance, Dan was punished by humiliation. Worse than having a newcomer's standing at the bottom of the social totem pole, he felt he had no standing whatsoever.

Humiliation is a difficult emotion to overcome, and public humiliation is worst of all. To use the example of the dog again, how would you expect the dog to act the next time that I say, "Fetch"? If you think the dog would display shaking, trembling, an inability to respond, and possible urination, you are correct. Dan's responses were similar. He was numb, basically incapacitated, and when he apologized, he participated in his own humiliation. It was as if his will were taken away. Usually, after such an experience, most people feel intense physical and emotional exhaustion. It will take more time for Dan to recoup emotionally than physically.

There are several proactive steps that Dan can try. First, Dan needs to evaluate the incident in a rational manner. He needs to evaluate Dr. Madson's intent. Dan should discuss the incident with an out-of-district mentor to gain an understanding of the group dynamics and release his own frustration. Second, he needs to learn more about district politics. Third, when Dan comes in contact with "club members," he should refer to the diner incident as his first celebrity roast. This is a subtle way to change their negative attitudes into acceptance. Finally, he needs to talk privately with Dr. Madson regarding his behavior at the diner. His silence would indicate to Dr. Madson that he would accept such treatment again. Dan needs to voice his objections.

ADDITIONAL SUGGESTIONS: WHAT ELSE COULD AND SHOULD YOU DO IN SIMILAR SITUATIONS?

Although a number of positive actions were demonstrated in this case, several additional suggestions to successfully survive this uncomfortable and potentially damaging situation are the following:

1. Do not overreact. In many situations, our view of what is embarrassing or humiliating might be skewed or inflated. Dan might have suffered much less if he viewed the situation as less serious or damaging. There is some question as to the gravity of this incident. One way to check your personal "read" or perspective of a given situation is to ask yourself the following questions: If I were a bystander and heard this transpire, would I feel sorry for the object of this roast? Did this ribbing damage the individual? If your answer is *no* to either of the above, relax and don't take the situation so seriously. However, if your answer is *yes*, proceed coolly, thoughtfully, and professionally.

2. Heed the advice of Robert Carlson (1997), "Surrender to the fact that life isn't fair" (p. 47). If you understand and accept Carlson's statement, it becomes much easier to proceed. Instead of expending needless energy bemoaning an injustice done to you, you can focus on your direction and behavior. Rodney LaBrecque (1998) urges us to think "Teflon." If you are covered in Teflon, the criticism will not stick but rather roll off and be discarded.

3. Take the time you need to calm yourself. Waiting to respond until you are reasonably calm most often increases your ability to respond intelligently and thoughtfully (Bailey, 1990). One useful calming technique is Jacobson's (1938) relaxation device: **Breathe in** for a three count; **hold** for three; **breathe out** for three; **hold** for three. Repeat until calm.

4. Determine the degree of truth or validity of the embarrassing or humiliating statements. Are the comments true, somewhat true, or completely erroneous? What was the degree of truth told? Your determination will likely dictate your response. If Superintendent Madson's remarks about Dan were technically correct, Dan could have said the following to lighten the situation: "He's absolutely right. It could have been a very difficult problem. I'm sure glad Clayton and I worked together to protect the district and still were able to deal successfully with the student. It's great to have a boss you can count on." If, however, Madson's remarks were somewhat twisted or only partially true, Dan Ortega might have responded,

"Now, Clayton, you know I was the one to call you. Now admit it. Aren't you glad I always call before suspending or expelling a student? Heck, you're the one who taught me that!" Finally, if the superintendent's accusation was completely false, Dan might have replied, "Gee, Clayton, that's not the way I remember it at all." There are times when, regardless of veracity, it is impossible to respond because of the need for confidentiality. In that situation, it is often possible to express your inability to respond. You might remark, "I'm afraid I can't agree, but for several reasons this is an inappropriate time and place to discuss this."

5. Consider the use of humor. Humor is a very powerful tool in tense situations such as embarrassment, ridicule, or humiliation. An old adage, as true today as it was for our grandparents, is "It is a big person who can laugh at himself." Isn't it better to have people laugh *with* you than *at* you?

6. Clear the air regarding potential litigation. At a later and more appropriate time, Dan should voice his concern to Dr. Madson regarding the legal ramifications of discussing a student, by name, in public. Although it seems ludicrous that a practicing superintendent would not understand that such behavior creates a grave and potentially litigious situation for himself and Dan, his behavior speaks otherwise. As a matter of self-preservation, Dan needs to voice his concern about and disapproval of such events in the future.

IN WHAT OTHER CASES DO THE LEARNED TECHNIQUES APPLY?

Public embarrassment, ridicule, or humiliation may come from a variety of sources. Any constituent is capable of such behavior. This form of verbal confrontation may be hurled at you from a superordinate, peer, constituent, or subordinate. As a professional, the suggestions provided above may be adapted to meet most situations. The key to success in every incident is to remain levelheaded, professional, and detached. Avoid retaliation and defensiveness (Charlesworth & Nathan, 1985; Kierkegaard, 1980; Schwartz, 1995).

SUMMARY

- The more responsibility and visibility people have, the more vulnerable they are to being embarrassed, ridiculed, or humiliated. School administrators have a great deal of responsibility and are highly visible. Therefore, expect that on occasion you will experience this taxing and often painful phenomenon.
- Cruel humiliation tactics often develop in childhood. Be prepared to confront and correct individuals who use these tactics. Success will be limited.
- Remember to keep things in perspective. Don't blow things out of proportion. Things might not actually be as damaging or serious as you first believe.
- Remain cool and positive. Learn to use relaxation techniques.
- Let the degree of "truth told" be a guide to your response.
- Learn to insert humor in your attitude and statements. Humor is a powerful weapon in your professional arsenal.

SUGGESTED READINGS

Learning About Attitudes and Techniques That Help When Embarrassed or Humiliated

Carlson, R. (1997). *Don't sweat the small stuff . . . and it's all small stuff.* New York: Hyperion.

Lee, J. (with Stott, B.). (1993). *Facing the fire: Experiencing and expressing anger appropriately.* New York: Bantam Books.

Schwartz, T. (1995). *What really matters?* New York: Bantam Books.

Learning About Multiple and Emotional Intelligences

Gardner, H. (1994). *The arts and human development.* New York: Basic Books.

Gardner, H. (1995). *Leading minds: An anatomy of leadership.* New York: Basic Books.

Goleman, D. (1998). *Emotional intelligence.* New York: Bantam.

Lazear, D. (1991). *Seven ways of knowing: Teaching for multiple intelligences* (2nd ed.). Palatine, IL: IRI/Skylight.

CHAPTER THREE

Handling Legitimate Complaints

THE STORY: Defending the Poor Teacher

THE PLACE: Upper-Class Urban Middle School

"**R**achel, I may be a few minutes late. Tell the physician assistant to cover for me if I don't get there on time." Dr. Margaret Spencer put her cellular phone back into her pocket. She drummed her fingers on the table next to her straight-backed chair and took another sip of the spring water the staff person had given her. The school's main office was busy with students and adults coming and going. She was not used to waiting and she was getting impatient. She needed to be at her medical clinic in 40 minutes. If the rolled-over semi was cleared away at "spaghetti junction," she still could make it on time. Did this principal think that parents had the time to wait in the middle of the afternoon?

At that moment, the principal, Dr. Penny Martin, entered from the main hallway. Dr. Martin, a tall, stately, and conservatively dressed woman, smiled as she invited Dr. Spencer into her office.

As soon as they had exchanged greetings and were seated, Dr. Spencer got right to the point. "Dr. Martin, I'm here because of David Grant, Rebecca Ann's math teacher. She said things about him I just don't like. She told her father and me that Mr. Grant punished her, along with the entire class, when she hadn't done anything wrong. I believe her. She feels that he is unfair and that he picks on her. He has a problem and I don't want him to be taking it out on my daughter. If there are a few children who need correction, then correct them, not Rebecca Ann."

Penny Martin was surprised that Margaret Spencer spoke so passionately. This was the first time she had heard of any problem between Mr. Grant, the sixth-grade accelerated-math teacher, and the Spencers. "Can you tell me any specific incidents that upset you? Exactly what happened to make you come to these conclusions?" asked Dr. Martin.

"It's a long story. Rebecca Ann has been upset all semester. She continually complains that Mr. Grant punishes the whole class when an individual child, usually Vicky Fisher, misbehaves. You know Rebecca is a good student. She loves math and has gotten A's all of her life. Now she cries about school and her grades have begun to drop. Something is very wrong. School should be fun, not misery," sputtered Margaret Spencer.

Without pausing, the angry mother continued, "I think you have an egomaniac on your hands who enjoys intimidating sensitive and impressionable preteens."

Not at all ruffled, Penny Martin queried, "Have you spoken directly with Mr. Grant about your concerns?"

Dr. Spencer snapped back, "Of course! What do you take me for? How dumb do you think I am? We've talked a number of times on the phone with the same results. Nothing! He kept saying this is a difficult age and the students needed a strong hand or else there would be chaos. He said something about preadolescence, lack of discipline, and hormones. Please! I don't need a pseudopsychiatrist lecturing me on hormones. My daughter doesn't deserve to be punished for things she hasn't done. On Monday, Rebecca Ann came home crying again. She said she doesn't like math and doesn't want to go to school. This is too much! I want that man stopped and I want you to do it!"

Penny Martin had heard this accusation before, but never with such virulence. Every year for the last seven years, one or two parents complained that David Grant was too demanding and that he unfairly punished the entire class for the behavior of one child. Here it was again.

Penny knew many things about David Grant. David had been in the school district for many years. He was 52 and one of the few remaining of the old guard since most of his compatriots took early retirement. Penny knew that after several failed attempts at other careers, David went back to school to get his teaching degree on the GI Bill. His ex-wife, Jennifer, was her friend. They had taken administration courses together. Jennifer never spoke ill of David, but when the opportunity to move up came, she took the job and divorced him. Since then, David had kept to himself. Occasionally he seemed depressed, but when asked, he denied any problems. He really did many things well, but sometimes he was heavy handed and unfair in the punishments he meted out to students.

For many years, Penny had publicly defended David's behavior and privately demanded a change in his management practices. For a while, things would be fine. Then, after a time, David Grant would revert to the same old behavior.

This was a serious dilemma. David Grant had wonderful credentials, his students performed extremely well on the required state test, and the school had no other certified math teacher to replace him. During a previous incident, when his classroom management style was questioned, he was able to produce parents who supported his methods.

Now Penny Martin had another parent complaining about David's overbearing "Gestapo" tactics. She decided to separate her problems. First, she would try to calm and placate Dr. Spencer, and then she would privately reprimand Mr. Grant. This technique had worked in the past situations. It most likely would work now. Penny desperately wanted this distressing situation to disappear.

Feeling uneasy, Penny sat quietly for a moment, then looked directly at Margaret Spencer and began, "I'm so surprised by your feelings. Over the years, parents have come to me with praise for Mr. Grant's ability to work with 12- and 13-year-olds. I must agree. I'm frequently in his classroom and regularly observe Mr. Grant. He's a fine teacher and I believe his treatment of children is fair. I agree that he does challenge them to grow, but he does so in a most appropriate fashion. I'm sure he wouldn't resort to negative consequences without just cause. I'd say he's one of our best. Perhaps Rebecca Ann is overreacting and highly sensitive at this time of her life."

Dr. Margaret Spencer was stunned. She had always liked Dr. Martin and thought her well qualified and honest. She never considered the possibility that Penny Martin would defend Mr. Grant, let alone praise him. Dr. Spencer felt betrayed. She had misjudged this principal. There would be no fair hearing from this woman. So be it!

Dr. Spencer swallowed, then coolly responded, "So, I take it you see no reason to pursue this matter further? It is your decision and you are the expert. I'm sure you have many other pressing problems, so I won't take up any more of your time."

"I appreciate your confidence in me and your sensible approach." said Penny Martin, secretly breathing a sigh of relief. "If you hear of any other incident, try to find out the details and get back to me. You know I'm here to help." Both women stood and stiffly said their goodbyes.

Alone, Penny Martin sank into her chair and cupped her head with both hands. She felt terrible. This was not a satisfactory way to handle a legitimate parent complaint. She felt guilty about the way she had manipulated Dr. Spencer. Penny decided to rethink her methods. How can a good administrator defend a teacher and at the same time protect the students?

As Dr. Margaret Spencer drove toward her medical clinic, she punched the speed dial on her cell phone and reached her receptionist. "Rachel, please find the number for the superintendent of the Evergreen School District and put it on my desk. I have some work to do."

HOW TAXING ARE SUCH ENCOUNTERS?

The surveyed school administrators who experienced situations where they had to protect and/or defend inappropriate or poor staff performance gave these encounters a **3–stressful** rating. They viewed this predicament as uncomfortable, irritating, and taxing. Practicing administrators felt that these types of situations were inherently stressful and distasteful. Most were unclear where their allegiance lay.

5–most stressful	4–more stressful	3– stressful	2–little stress	1–no stress

A PSYCHOLOGICAL PERSPECTIVE OF THIS SITUATION: WHAT DO WE KNOW ABOUT THE EMOTIONAL TOLL THIS SITUATION PLACED ON PENNY?

We all have a range of stress that we can manage while maintaining our physical and emotional health. We have many different roles that place demands upon us. The most important roles are those in our families, our jobs, and our friendships. We attempt to maintain a certain level of stasis in each of these situations. However, there are times when the balance is shifted by the weight of our responsibilities. The greater the weights on one side of the balance, the greater the impact on us physically and emotionally.

Let's posit that Penny's private life was in stasis. Her vocational life was in stasis until Dr. Spencer walked into her office. Dr. Spencer expressed concern for her daughter and the treatment that she was receiving from her math teacher. She directly expressed her belief based upon her daughter's statements that David Grant was abusing his students. He habitually punished the whole class for the misbehavior of one student. This was a patently inappropriate behavior. Dr. Spencer came to Penny with the hope of alleviating her concerns for her daughter and rectifying the classroom situation.

In response to Dr. Spencer's overture, Penny avoided the truth and placed the burden back upon the unfortunate and innocent student. She did not face the reality of her situation but, rather, deluded herself with the belief that she could avoid confrontation with David and appease Dr. Spencer. Her lack of courage made her situation worse. She added the weights of an angry, influential parent; the upset student; the fact that David's behavior will lead to other confrontations; and the knowledge of her own failings.

By doing so, Penny shifted her emotional and physical balance in a negative direction. She was no longer in stasis, or balance.

Physiologically, the consequences are not readily apparent for most people. What we don't see *can* hurt us. For some people, there are psychophysiological reactions such as essential hypertension, irritable bowel syndrome, temporomandibular (TMJ) problems, headaches, and dermatological disorders (Gatchel & Blanchard, 1993). Many people don't associate these symptoms with their poor decision making, but there is often a direct relationship.

Emotionally, the consequences for Penny were more apparent. She dealt with the situation with fear, avoidance, and indecisiveness. This resulted in diminished capacity for effective work. She made a personal hell for herself that will demand a day of reckoning. We can be assured that Dr. Spencer will not rest until she is vindicated, even if it means lobbying for Penny's removal.

HOW WELL DID THE PRINCIPAL DEFEND THE TEACHER WITH QUESTIONABLE PRACTICES?

A Practitioner's View

Ouch! Dr. Martin handled this incident poorly. She did not behave as an instructional leader. Community relations skills were sorely lacking. Integrity was nonexistent. She did not shoulder her responsibilities to the students, the concerned parent, the misguided teacher, or the educational program.

Principal Martin treated Dr. Spencer in a demeaning and insulting manner. Although she feigned cordiality and politeness, she clearly took a superior and condescending posture. She gave the impression that this parent's concerns were ungrounded, frivolous, and fallacious. Penny Martin was patronizing.

Dr. Spencer came to school with legitimate and serious concerns and was told they were blown out of proportion. She deserved better! Community support is crucial to the survival of good schools. Dr. Martin's practices undermined any positive school community relations efforts (Hansen & Childs, 1998; Riley, 1996; SuiChu & Willm, 1996).

Although Dr. Martin provided Dr. Spencer with an opportunity to voice her concerns, she deliberately lied to her. Penny Martin knew from past experience that David Grant used damaging disciplinary practices. She was sure that the parent's complaints were true. Yet, she deliberately lied to Dr. Spencer about Mr. Grant's reputation and performance. Furthermore, in their conversation, Dr. Martin unfairly shifted the "blame" to Rebecca Ann. In short, Dr. Penny Martin's conversation and treatment of the Spencers were both unprofessional and reprehensible. These behaviors are not the ones expected in a positive school climate (Glasser, 1997; Kelly et al., 1998).

Principal Martin also failed in her duties to Mr. Grant. We learned in this scenario that David Grant, over many years, had used questionable discipline tactics. Who is to blame? Dr. Martin must accept some responsibility for Mr. Grant's poor performance. Only talking to him was a Band-Aid approach, when what was needed was true proactive action. This was a disservice to David. She should have provided him with professional development training in classroom management. If professional development training was ineffective, Dr. Martin should have utilized remediation. Better no teacher than one who scars learners for life.

This vignette suggested that Dr. Martin failed the students and the goals of the school's educational program. It is the responsibility of the principal to cultivate a positive learning environment (Kosmoski & Pollack, 1997). By not acting positively to change an appalling classroom situation, Penny cheated the students of a positive and nurturing climate where learning occurs. Her failure to take the tough but necessary action ultimately affected the students.

Finally, Dr. Martin deluded herself with the belief that, regardless of the circumstances, it was necessary to protect the staff. Any educator who has read the effective schools research of the 1980s and 1990s learned that teachers demand that administrators publicly support their efforts. Teachers work more effectively if school administrators defend and support them against false accusations (Acheson & Gall, 1992; Kosmoski & Pollack, 1997). Dr. Martin made the common mistake of misinterpreting these findings. She believed that it was her duty to defend Mr. Grant's actions regardless of how inhumane and ineffective they were. The research clearly states that teachers can rightfully expect an instructional leader to support and defend them against false, unjust, and improper accusations or allegations. However, teachers neither expect nor want administrators to protect their unfit colleagues (Barr & Tagg, 1995; Illinois Federation of Teachers, 1999; Nelson, 1998; Spring, 1991). In this case, the teacher's actions were wrong and did not merit blanket protection. Teacher support should not be equated with cover-up. Dr. Martin's obligation was first to her students and then to David Grant. She should not have sacrificed student needs and rights for an unfounded and false loyalty to a faculty member.

Wade Nelson (1998) eloquently explains the grave responsibility we have to provide students with the best teachers possible when he states, "As our largest public institution, public education is the epicenter of a struggle for the control of the hearts and minds of the next generation" (p. 684). Students perform best when they are respected, expected to succeed, and encouraged and praised when they stretch (Fried, 1995; Kosmoski & Pollack, 1997; Lasley, 1998).

A Clinical View

Most of us would be abashed if we were approached by our principal and reprimanded for our behavior. We know that Dr. Martin in the past had discussed Mr. Grant's problems with him. Also, she had evidence of some parental support. Penny praised his abilities and criticized his limitations. Her actions did not cause a change in Mr. Grant's behavior.

Why would David behave this way? What Penny knew about him might provide an answer. She knew that he was 52 years old. After several career changes, he obtained his degree on the GI Bill. David was divorced with two children who lived with their mother. Penny knew his ex-wife and was surprised when she filed for divorce. David was a quiet man who kept to himself. Other than David Grant's insensitivity to students, Penny knew of no events in his career that had brought him notoriety. She attributed his occasional morose demeanor to his loss of family.

David's history and numerous behaviors point to the possibility of Posttraumatic Stress Disorder (PTSD). PTSD frequently leads to difficulty with interpersonal relationships, marital conflict, divorce, and job loss (American Psychiatric Association, 1994). Victims have difficulty modulating their feelings and are self-destructive, dissociative, and socially withdrawn. They feel constantly threatened and experience impaired relationships with others. The incidence rate of PTSD is between 1% and 14% in a community's population. Penny Martin needed to be sensitive to this Vietnam vet's possible PTSD. She should have referred him to a qualified professional.

ADDITIONAL SUGGESTIONS:
WHAT ELSE COULD AND SHOULD
YOU DO IN SIMILAR SITUATIONS?

1. One role of the school administrator is to manage concerns, complaints, and accusations. Some are genuine and some false. Until resolved, *all* should be taken seriously. They are all legitimate and valid until proven otherwise. School administrators need to adopt this position when dealing with similar situations (Simonelli, 1996).

2. In these encounters, the operative word is document. Document, document, and document! Document the concern, complaint, or accusation. Inform the claimant that you are documenting his or her statement. One might take notes or tape-record (tape-recording is intimidating, so move cautiously). After a conversation is documented, have the party verbally verify your entries. For example, after obtaining permission to take notes of a complaint conversation, read your notes back to all parties for verification and accuracy. This practice virtually eliminates later disclaimers or denials. Documentation successfully discourages insincere complaints and supports just claims.

3. When the solution to a problem is evident and you have direct knowledge of it, share it directly with the concerned party. Sometimes, added information can immediately defuse a potential powder keg. You can straighten out a tangled web of information with simple clear facts.

4. If the situation requires more information, gather it. Offer to find out more and report back. Then do it! Report your findings. This might entail contacting the involved individuals. It may also require that you have additional meetings that include the accused party. One illustration might be parents who accuse a teacher of picking on their child. Check out the circumstances, and then arrange a later meeting with the teacher, parents, and you, as mediator.

5. Last, remember your primary purpose. You are there to rectify and resolve problems. It is not a situation that attacks you. You are not the focal point. You are a problem solver and mediator. This is not about you and your feelings. Keep these facts foremost in your mind.

IN WHAT OTHER CASES DO THE LEARNED TECHNIQUES APPLY?

There is a myriad of scenarios where the school administrator must resolve constituents' concerns and complaints. Community members, parents, staff, and students will approach you. Usually, they are sincere and serious. They trust your honesty, efficiency, and sincerity. As a school administrator, you are obliged to treat them with respect. Although you are swamped with the daily grind, you must find the time and give the effort. These practices will cement your place in the internal and external community. It will also provide you with a vehicle to monitor present conditions, improve school image, and rectify substandard practices. Good techniques and solid practices are also applicable when working with students and adults (Cohan & Lotan, 1995; Freiberg, 1998).

SUMMARY

- Consider all complaints or accusations as serious and valid until proven otherwise. Respect the individual who came to you with concerns and understand that, for most people, this is not an easy situation.
- Promptly rectify any valid misunderstanding or complaint of which you have accurate direct knowledge. Ignoring the situation or settling for a quick but temporary fix will only cause additional difficulties.
- Do not equate staff support with blind blanket protection. Teachers do not expect you to protect a "rotten apple."
- Document complaints. Documentation is critical for clarity and to prevent later disclaimers or denials. Be sure the individual making a charge knows you are documenting remarks.
- Gather additional information when needed. On some occasions, resolution or rectification requires collecting pertinent information. Get all the salient facts before making a judgment.
- Involve necessary key players. This might include staff, students, parents, and community members.
- Do not feel threatened when an individual lodges a complaint or voices an accusation. By coming to you, it implies

that the person respects and trusts you. Use this situation as an opportunity for improvement, rather than as a defensive stand (Peterson & Deal, 1998).

- Use these suggestions when dealing with allegations both within and outside the school setting. These techniques are useful with adults and students.
- Remember that parents play an essential part in the success of an educational program. They provide needed input, public support, and volunteer service. They can be the school's best friends (Cavarretta, 1998; Gladwell, 1998; Olson, 1998).

SUGGESTED READINGS

Beaudoin, M., & Taylor, M. (2004). *Creating a positive school culture: How principals and teachers can solve problems together.* Thousand Oaks, CA: Corwin.

Freiberg, H. J. (1998). Measuring school climate: Let me count the ways. *Educational Leadership, 56*(1), 22–27.

Fried, R. (1995). *The passionate teacher.* Boston: Beacon Press.

Georgia Department of Education. (1993–2003). Building a positive school environment. Retrieved July 2004 from www.ascd.org/cms/index.cfm?theViewID=1945

Glasser, W. (1997). A new look at school failure and school success. *Phi Delta Kappan, 78*(8), 596–602.

Hansen, J. M., & Childs, J. (1998). Creating a school where people like to be. *Educational Leadership, 56*(1), 14–17.

Kelly, P. A., Brown, S., Butler, A., Pelah, G., Taylor, C., & Zeller, P. (1998). A place to hang our hats. *Educational Leadership, 56*(1), 62–64.

Peterson. K. D., & Deal, T. E. (1998). How leaders influence the culture of schools. *Educational Leadership, 56*(1), 28–31.

Simonelli, R. (1996, Winter). The basic school: Recreating community for educational development. *Winds of Change, 11*(1), 22–25.

Sizer, T. R. (1992). *Horace's school.* Boston: Houghton Mifflin.

U. S. Department of Education. (2004). Creating a positive school climate. Retrieved July 2004 from www.edu.gov.mb.ca/ks4/specedu/fas/pdf/3.pdf

CHAPTER FOUR

Controlling
Those Under
the Influence

THE STORY: Flying High: A Collision Course With Disaster

THE PLACE: Middle- to Upper-Class, Multiethnic Suburbia

A t 9:30 a.m. on Tuesday, Dr. Judy Blake, principal of Lincoln Elementary, was sipping her second cup of coffee and returning calls in her office when her secretary, Pat, burst in without knocking. Usually a calm and controlled person, Pat's face and body language signaled fear and big trouble. Judy Blake immediately cut short her phone call by simply saying, "Something important has just come up. I'll get right back to you."

Hanging up the phone, Judy jumped out of her chair and swiftly moved toward the door. "What's going on?" she demanded. Pat sputtered, "Amanda Gireaux's mother just stormed in, pushed me aside, and is heading down the hall to Mrs. Gonzales's room!"

Judy remembered the woman. She was tall, bony, and a bit rough around the edges, but just last week Judy had watched her tenderly hug her daughter when she dropped her off for school. Judy decided that Mrs. Gireaux probably didn't understand the school rules. She smiled and said, "It's okay. I'll find her and take care of it."

"No! You don't understand. She says she's 'going to teach that little shit the lesson of her life.' Judy, she almost knocked me down. She's headed toward the fifth-grade wing of the building and . . . and she reeks of whiskey."

This news hit Judy like a lead fist. She realized instantly that the situation was very serious. Alcohol and anger are main ingredients in the recipe for violence. Her students and teachers could be in genuine danger. Heart pounding and stomach in knots, her mind raced. Already in the hall, she turned back to Pat and the other office personnel who had gathered and said, "Call the police. I'm going after her. Send help when they come. Be sure to tell them not to use their siren. My goal is to get her out of the building before anyone gets hurt."

Judy hurried as she rounded the last corner of the hall leading to the fifth-grade classrooms. She slowed to a walk, took a deep breath, and quickly scanned the hallway. Taking in the scene, she was relieved to find the area virtually empty. No children were in sight. She could hear Mrs. Gireaux yelling at Mrs. Gonzales, Lincoln's veteran fifth-grade teacher. Thank goodness Mrs. Gonzales was standing between the screaming woman and the classroom door. Towering over the teacher, the threatening mother was demanding the teacher produce her child so that she could "whip her good."

At that point, the two women must have heard Judy's heels clicking on the tiles as she approached them. Their heads snapped in her direction and both women stared at her. It was a good sign; she had their full attention.

Trying to appear friendly yet concerned, Judy looked directly at the sweaty, glassy-eyed intruder. Yes, she smelled of liquor and was very agitated and very angry. Smiling slightly, Judy stepped in front of the teacher, faced Mrs. Gireaux, and began in a steady, low voice. "Hello, Mrs. Gireaux. I'm Judy Blake, the principal." Judy extended her arm, offering to shake hands. Without thinking, Mrs. Gireaux responded and took the proffered handshake. Continuing to hold the woman's hand while placing her free hand on her wrist, Judy continued, "I understand you have a problem this morning. You've come to the right person. I think I might be able to help you. Let's see if we can find a better place to talk and we can work this out."

Over her shoulder, Judy addressed the teacher, "Mrs. Gonzales, you and your students need to return to your work now. Mrs. Gireaux no longer needs your help. I'll assist her."

Mrs. Gonzales smoothly took the cue, nodded agreement, and stepped into her room. She waved the wide-eyed children who crowded the entrance back to their seats and firmly closed the door behind her. This left Mrs. Gireaux and Judy alone in the hall. Goal one accomplished: no daughter, no fellow students, and no teachers directly in the line of fire.

Lightly touching the woman's forearm, Judy guided Mrs. Gireaux back toward the front entrance. As they slowly walked, Judy Blake began asking questions in a conversational tone, "May I call you by your first name? What has Amanda done to upset you, Mrs. Gireaux?" and "What can we do to help?" As Mrs. Gireaux spoke, Judy stayed close beside her and nodded at the appropriate times.

As they reached the main doors, Judy suggested that, since it was a beautiful day, the two of them get some needed fresh air. She gently steered the heavily intoxicated woman outdoors. As they talked, Judy was careful to agree with the woman as much as possible. She knew she was more concerned with demeanor and emotional climate than logic and problem solving.

After a few minutes, a squad car sped up the front drive. As it approached, Mrs. Gireaux wheeled on Judy. "You, blonde, boney-ass bitch! You called the cops on me!"

"No, Mrs. Gireaux. I called the police before I knew it was you. I was afraid for the safety of the children, and my first thought was of protecting them. Trust me. I'll explain to the officers that you had come to visit your daughter. I'll take care of this," Judy responded calmly.

Judy greeted the two officers as they stepped out of the car. Alice Gireaux's demeanor quickly changed; her bravado notice-ably diminished. Pulling the police officers aside, Judy explained that Mrs. Gireaux had been very upset earlier but was now feeling much calmer. She insisted that it would neither be wise nor safe for Mrs. Gireaux to drive at the present time. Judy then asked if the policemen would kindly take her home.

After introducing the officers to Alice Gireaux, there was some discussion about ways to collect her car and scheduling an appointment with Judy later in the week. After again shaking hands, Mrs. Gireaux surprised Judy by giving her a brief hug and then left meekly with the officers.

The whole event had taken no more than 10 minutes. Shaken, Dr. Judy Blake took a long breath, let out a sigh of relief, ruefully acknowledged her trembling knees, and offered up a small prayer of thanksgiving.

HOW TAXING ARE SUCH ENCOUNTERS?

Confrontations in schools with adults or students who are under the influence of drugs or alcohol are viewed as among the most stressful encounters experienced by the practicing school administrator. Understandable. Common sense tells us that out-of-control and, therefore, irrational people pose a real physical threat to all. Fear of this kind of danger is not only normal but desirable. The 250 polled practicing school administrators rated this type of encounter as **5–most stressful.**

5–most stressful	4–more stressful	3– stressful	2–little stress	1–no stress

A PSYCHOLOGICAL PERSPECTIVE OF THIS SITUATION: WHAT DO WE KNOW ABOUT PEOPLE WHO ARE UNDER THE INFLUENCE OF DRUGS OR ALCOHOL?

People under the influence of drugs present many problems for society. In our daily lives, we are often victims of people who are under the influence of drugs or alcohol. Imagine yourself in these three situations. You go to the emergency room and are treated by a young doctor high on narcotics. He obtained the drugs by writing his own prescription. Would you want to be treated by such a physician? Or, imagine that you are involved in a personal injury lawsuit. Your lead attorney and her partner ask for a brief recess. The three of you meet in a conference room. As soon as the door closes, the partner tells your attorney that her arguments are flawed and that she needs to quit snorting cocaine every morning before the start of court. Would you want such an attorney?

Finally, imagine yourself working in a restaurant and a former coworker comes into the place brandishing a knife. He demands the night receipts because he needs money for methamphetamines. He apologizes for what he is about to do. Your "friend" slits the cashier's throat and seconds later yours. You and the cashier die. He is sentenced to death for both murders.

All three are true stories. All three cases had terrible consequences for the drug users, as well as their victims.

After the fact, we wouldn't care that the physician became addicted because of migraine headaches, or that the attorney became addicted after her spouse bought her cocaine for a birthday present, or that, from the age of nine, the murderer was given drugs by his amphetamine-addicted mother. However, we do care what these people did while under the influence of drugs.

Similarly, in the case of Mrs. Gireaux, we don't care why she drinks. Whatever the cause, she was a potential threat to Amanda and the other students because the alcohol affected her judgment.

Mrs. Gireaux burst into the school and obviously acted inappropriately. Judy confirmed with her own nose that Mrs. Gireaux had been drinking. This gave Judy a sense of relief. Sure, the intruder was angry and agitated, but now Judy had valuable information at her disposal. She knew the psychological and physiological effects of alcohol, and she had some knowledge of this parent as an individual. Mrs. Gireaux really wished to allay her own fears and anxiety, not to threaten others. Judy knew Mrs. Gireaux's behaviors were antithetical to the effects of alcohol. Mrs. Gireaux was angry and agitated, whereas alcohol is a depressant. By acting in a calm and soothing manner, Judy helped Mrs. Gireaux put her emotions and physiology in sync. Judy Blake was able to help this raging parent change her behaviors and reach her desired state of momentary well-being. Finally, Judy Blake understood that Mrs. Gireaux was not likely to remember any of this encounter.

HOW WELL DID THE PRINCIPAL HANDLE THE PARENT WHO WAS FLYING HIGH?

A Practitioner's View

Judy Blake's overall behavior in this situation should be commended. Most noteworthy among her actions were the correct recognition and assessment of a potentially dangerous situation, identification and proper ordering of the most crucial actions necessary to defuse the event, speedy response time, and communication skills.

Assessment of the Situation. As soon as the facts became clear, Judy recognized the very serious nature of the matter. She immediately understood that an intoxicated, angry, physically menacing adult can inflict grave injury to students and staff. Simpson (1998) reminds us that we must take threats seriously. Judy Blake knew that Mrs. Gireaux needed to be stopped and removed from the premises as quickly and peaceably as possible. She exemplified the behaviors of an effective leader described by Morrison, White, and Van Velsor: "She doesn't fall apart when things get tough. She has great cool under pressure" (1987, p. 24).

Execution of Appropriate Actions. This principal successfully executed a remarkable series of correct behaviors. First, she arranged for help. By instructing her secretary to notify the police, she ensured backup or, if it became necessary, the force required to terminate this threat. It took courage for Judy to order the police call. Too often and for too many reasons, school administrators avoid calling for help. Some misguided administrators don't want to appear foolish if the call turns out to be unnecessary. Law enforcement experts constantly assure us that it is better to call in 10 false alarms than to fail to make the one call that is necessary. Other administrators harbor the false notion that calling the police will give their school "a black eye"; it will damage the school's reputation and jeopardize good community relations. This is an untenable position. Experts in community relations have identified school safety and climate issues as among the most important with parents and community members (Estep, 2003; Kohn, 1996; Rose & Gallup, 2003; Schmidt, 1997).

Judy showed exceptional dedication and courage by immediately going to the scene herself. She demonstrated the principle of early intervention stressed by conflict resolution experts who advise that we act as soon as possible (Estep, 2003; Render, Padilla, & Krank, 1989; Stone, Patton, Heen, & Fisher, 2000; Toby, 1993–1994; Wilson, 1995). She accurately prioritized her own behaviors by removing the vulnerable students and staff from the situation. Dr. Blake then had better control of events and contained the confrontation between Mrs. Gireaux and herself. By physically shifting the action down the hall and out the door, Judy literally removed the threat from Lincoln School. Finally, by pacifying Mrs. Gireaux regarding police intervention and by obtaining her cooperation, Judy may have eliminated future reprisals and perhaps initiated the first step toward healing.

Response Time. Judy Blake's speedy action speaks for itself. Throughout this affair, Judy acted both decisively and swiftly. Both qualities are essential in potentially dangerous situations. School administrators could use Judy's reaction time as a model when faced with such predicaments. Some examples of excellent use of time included going into action as soon as she saw her secretary's unusual behaviors and worry, requesting police support, moving physically between the teacher and the mother, and exiting the building with the angry drunken parent.

Communication Skills. Throughout this event, Principal Blake demonstrated excellent communication skills. Her verbal ability and body language were assets for her. One praiseworthy skill was her ability to speak calmly yet firmly when giving directions to staff. She addressed the issue insightfully, disregarding irrelevant data and getting directly to the central components. The same was true when she responded to Mrs. Gireaux's reaction to the arrival of the police.

Judy also used superb delivery skills while speaking with all participants. She kept her volume low and tone conversational, never yelling or demanding. She conveyed self-control and professionalism. Judy's tone and volume must have conveyed understanding, acceptance, and trustworthiness to Mrs. Gireaux.

Judy's body language during this situation helped to achieve a positive resolution. One example included stepping between Mrs. Gireaux, on one side, and the teacher, classroom, and children on the other side. Another example was making nonthreatening physical contact by shaking hands before the actual dialogue and maintaining that contact throughout the episode. Remember the subtle cues she used when engaged with Mrs. Gireaux: she smiled, looked directly into the mother's eyes, and nodded. These are all techniques advocated for active listening (Panico, 1999).

A Clinical View

Dr. Blake managed the entire situation quite well. Rather than confront Mrs. Gireaux, Judy started with a question, "How can I help you?" This question engages the angry person without being threatening. It allows the transgressor to see the principal as a means to achieving her own purposes rather than as a guard or gatekeeper.

Would Mrs. Gireaux respond to another person in the same way? Would a male parent have reacted in the same way to Judy? Maybe or maybe not. Although it is impossible to predict, a nonthreatening, helpful posture is usually a good starting point with all people.

What about Judy's touching Mrs. Gireaux? It is not threatening for a female to be touched by another female. Rather, it is often viewed as soothing and supportive. So, in this case, it was very appropriate behavior on Judy's part. However, be aware that being touched by a person of the opposite sex or of another ethnicity is frequently perceived as threatening. Therefore, touching should generally be avoided during trying situations.

Did the police need to be called? Yes. Judy could not leave students at risk. She needed someone to physically manage Mrs. Gireaux, had the situation become violent. The police were a necessary safety backup. Judy and Mrs. Gireaux knew each other and their relationship was amicable. This made the situation more predictable and easier to control. If this were not the case, it would have been impossible for Judy to accurately predict a stranger's reactions.

In this situation, the police did not attempt to take control. This could only occur because Judy had developed a good working relationship with the local police, and they had come to trust her judgment. If she had not established a working relationship with the local police, their behavior may have been different. Rather than agreeing to take Mrs. Gireaux home, they may have been more inclined to take her to jail or to wait with her until a family member came to take her home. Regardless of which scenario developed, it was best that Mrs. Gireaux was removed from the building.

Would Dr. Blake's behaviors be appropriate in both an urban or rural environment? Yes. Regardless of geographic location, the priorities remain the same. Protection of the school community and defusing of the situation must be the primary duty of the school administrator.

ADDITIONAL SUGGESTIONS: WHAT ELSE COULD AND SHOULD YOU DO IN SIMILAR SITUATIONS?

Although Dr. Judy Blake did an excellent job at Lincoln Elementary, reflection and brainstorming with successful and experienced administrators provide a number of additional suggestions to improve the odds for a positive resolution.

1. Lincoln School was very lucky that its principal was in the perfect position to take action. Emergencies do not always occur at convenient times. Before you are faced with this or a similar situation, it would be wise to determine a plan or procedure for quickly locating you or your second-in-command. Questions such as, Who should be contacted if there is an intruder? In what order should responsible individuals be located and mobilized? and When should authorities be summoned? should be addressed. Answers specific to you and your school should be clarified and widely disseminated. Armistead (1996) and Moriarity, Maeyama, and Fitzgerald (1993) urge all school administrators to develop and implement a crisis communication plan before violence occurs.

2. With the advent of zero tolerance policies, include a section in your student and parent handbooks that addresses the issue of being under the influence of drugs and alcohol. Your district and school should have written guidelines that clearly define procedures and practices to be followed if an individual is under, or suspected to be under, the influence of drugs or alcohol. Clear and widely distributed written policies protect your school and district from perpetrators who wish to retaliate, as well as from confrontational individuals and groups (Shanker, 1995).

3. One danger not satisfactorily addressed in this scenario was the lack of a plan to remove students from harm's way. Developing a plan for surreptitiously informing staff of a potentially dangerous intruder can effectively thwart danger even on short notice. It could be a two-short-bells warning or perhaps a public address announcement that "Mr. Crabtree is to report to the Loading Zone." The word *Crabtree* serves as the warning and order to mobilize. Upon receiving the warning, teachers should have a predetermined plan for directing students to a supervised

and safe location until the situation is resolved and the order is withdrawn.

4. Safety, now and in the future, for Mrs. Gireaux's daughter and any other siblings must be considered. If Mrs. Gireaux was so threatening in the public school, what might be going on in the privacy of her home? Are the Gireaux children safe? Is child abuse a possibility? There are a number of actions to consider. First, you have a legal and ethical duty to protect children by reporting any suspicions to the proper authorities. School administrators are bound by law to act on the part of their students. Prudent administrators work closely with local social service agents to ensure prompt and appropriate safeguards. Second, consider assigning a responsible adult to accompany the child home for the purpose of assessing the domestic climate. Does the home appear calm and safe? Finally, begin keeping a log that charts Mrs. Gireaux's actions.

5. Document the incident. An inherent problem when dealing with someone who is alcohol dependent, or at least alcohol abusive, is the possibility of blackouts. Blackouts are periods when an intoxicated person has no memory of events. If all of the activity in this vignette occurred during a blackout, Mrs. Gireaux would not be likely to remember the events the following day. Therefore, to protect the school and yourself, you must have some record of the incident in the office. A "Mrs. Gireaux" is likely to deny that the events of the previous day occurred even when she discovers her car in the school parking lot the next day.

6. If you have been remiss in establishing a positive and close relationship with the local police department, begin now. Their prompt response to a call for help, their perceptions of your ability to act correctly and decisively, and their input and involvement in the school are vital to effectively safeguarding students and creating positive community support.

7. Finally, this incident reminds us that the school campus is no longer a safe haven. It is no longer sacred. Rather, the climate in American schools is becoming more violent (Michigan Department of Education, 2000; U. S. Department of Education, 2004a; U. S. Department of Education, 2004b). Sadly, cases of student and adult violence in schools are reported on the national news. Since such an encounter could happen in any school, administrators should study

their existing security arrangements and, where necessary, strengthen them. The use of buzzer systems at entrances, security guards, and metal detectors must be seriously considered. These precautions might not have stopped Mrs. Gireaux, but then again, they might be just the deterrents that work.

IN WHAT OTHER CASES DO THE LEARNED TECHNIQUES APPLY?

The problem of drugs or alcohol is not confined to a school's unwanted visitors. Good administrators must understand that either by deliberate indulgence or by accident, all members of the school community—parents, staff, superordinates, and even small children—are vulnerable. Any time an individual's judgment is altered or impaired, he or she becomes a genuine danger to self and others. Knowing the telltale signs of this condition and the possible bizarre behaviors that might result are necessities for the school administrator. Finally, understanding appropriate countermeasures and possessing the resolve to act will go a long way toward ensuring a safe school environment (U.S. Department of Education, 2004a).

SUMMARY

If you confront an individual on your school campus who appears to be under the influence of drugs or alcohol, you should

- Understand that this is one of the most potentially hostile, dangerous, and stressful situations you will face as a school administrator. Take the encounter seriously.
- Strive to isolate the impaired, out-of-control individual from others. You need to remove the individual from the building and protect the school population until the danger has passed.
- When the situation warrants, summon police officers to help with the removal of the individual.
- Formulate an action plan. Act decisively and swiftly. Remember, prior reflection and established procedures can greatly reduce the danger.

- Use all the communication skills at your command. Both verbal and nonverbal skills are crucial. Engage in calm, professional, and caring behaviors. A quiet voice, a pleasant face, slow motions, and sometimes a gentle touch are most often useful.
- After the crisis has passed, consider supportive follow-up. Students and staff who have been involved in or even heard about a hostile confrontation might be distraught. Supportive and caring follow-up is appropriate leadership behavior.

SUGGESTED READINGS

Preparing for Dangerous People
Under the Influence of Drugs or Alcohol

Curwin, R. L., & Mendler, A. N. (1997). *School violence prevention.* Alexandria, VA: Association for Supervision and Curriculum Development.

Lichtenstein, R., Schonfield, D., Kline, M., & Spree-Licham, D. (1995). *How to prepare for and respond to a crisis.* Alexandria, VA: Association for Supervision and Curriculum Development.

United States Department of Education. (2004). *Crime and safety in America's public schools: Selected findings from the school survey on crime and safety.* Retrieved July 2004 from www.ed.gov/about/offices/list/osdfs/index.html [Education ID: NCES 2004–370. Note: Download is free.]

Learning About People and Substance Abuse

Hartmann, D. (1995). *Neuropsychological toxicology: Identification and assessment of human neurotoxic syndromes.* New York: Plenum.

Landry, M. J. (1994). *Understanding drug abuse: The process of addiction, treatment, and recovery.* Washington, DC: Psychiatric Press.

Lewis, J. A., Dana, R. Q., & Blevins, G. A. (1994). *Substance abuse counseling: An individual approach* (2nd ed.). New York: Simon & Schuster.

Ludwig, A. M. (1988). *Understanding the alcoholic's mind.* New York: Oxford University Press.

Updating Your Knowledge
Base About School Violence

Angels of Columbine Website. (2004). *School Violence link.* Retrieved June 2004 from http://www.columbine-angels.com

Refusing to Be Coerced

> THE STORY: Pressured by the Unethical Boss
>
> THE PLACE: Washington High School in a Suburb of a Large New England City

Jessica Chang heard the superintendent's voice from the outer office. After a few seconds, there was a brief knock and the door swung open. There stood Susan Anne Viper, superintendent of schools and Jessica's new boss. Susan Anne rarely waited to be announced. As usual, she was carrying an armload of papers and a huge appointment book.

After dropping most of her belongings on a side chair, the superintendent threw a large manila folder onto the round table in the corner of the room and took a seat. Somewhat frenzied, Susan Anne dove right in. "Well, good morning. How's my newest principal today? Can you believe that it's already November?"

Jessica opened her mouth, but before she could respond, Susan Anne continued, "Well, I hope you're ready for our first real evaluation meeting concerning your performance. I don't have a lot of time so we need to get right at this. I have two more building stops after this and need to keep on schedule."

Carrying her own folder, Jessica smiled and joined her boss at the table. Of course she was prepared for this meeting. Susan Anne's secretary had called and arranged the appointment about two weeks before. After speaking with another district principal, Jessica had a good idea of what to expect. She had been told that Susan Anne would arrive with a narrative report of her view of Jessica's performance. She would refer to the goals and objectives that Jessica had developed and she had approved for this school year. Susan Anne would expect a progress report that covered every objective and the specific activities used to accomplish each. Jessica heard that this meeting could go on for several hours and that Susan Anne Viper would be brutally frank and candid.

And so it began. Both women worked diligently and professionally. They covered a myriad of topics and areas of performance. To Jessica's delight, after only one hour and fifteen minutes, the meeting seemed to be wrapping up. Superintendent Viper was thorough, questioned a few actions, and mentioned some incidents where she approved of Jessica's actions. Positives far outweighed negatives. Although Susan Anne was not very warm, complimentary, or effusive, Jessica felt her comments were, by and large, fair and accurate. Jessica believed this was a great meeting. It was much better than she had hoped. It was a miracle! She hadn't been raked over the coals and the superintendent actually encouraged her to keep up the good work.

As the two women were sorting the pile of documentation, Susan Anne turned to Jessica and said, "You know, it's very nice to have an administrator I can count on in the district. I know you've been here only four months and already a number of your fellow principals are singing your praises. I even hear that a few regularly call you for advice and help." Jessica murmured her thanks and wondered how Susan Anne knew that her peers were seeking her out for direction or calling her to blow off steam.

Susan Anne leaned closer to Jessica and used a quiet, conspiratorial tone. "Not all our principals are as effective as you. I worry about them. I'm afraid they will get into real trouble before I hear about it or am able to help them. Because I'm the boss, some are afraid to be open or come to me with their problems. I need early, firsthand information about all my principals and assistants. Jessica, I'd like you to be my eyes and ears. Keep me informed. Tell me what they're up to."

Jessica Chang was dumbfounded and appalled. She felt a tight band around her chest. Her mind raced. Susan Anne Viper, her boss, was asking her to spy on her new colleagues and friends. She was trying to coerce Jessica with her position and bribing her with the promise of camaraderie.

What should she do? If she agreed, the superintendent would be satisfied and grateful. She would surely get excellent evaluations during the critical first year on the job. Susan Anne would treat her as a coconspirator and "friend." Yet, what escalation would Susan Anne want next? This was something she felt was unethical and something she could not do without feeling very guilty. She would consider herself a traitor and spy.

On the other hand, if she refused, she would certainly alienate her superior. In the short time Jessica had known her, she had learned that Susan Anne did not take *no* for an answer. Anyone who refused paid dearly. Still, Jessica had made a commitment to herself to stay true to her beliefs and standards of behavior. Being a stool pigeon for the boss was not a level to which she would sink. Jessica Chang decided to do what she felt was right and hope the consequences would be less than she feared.

"Susan Anne," Jessica replied, "I really can't agree to that. All my professional life I have honored confidences. Anything you tell me or share with me stays between us. The same holds true for my teachers and fellow principals. I would never repeat what was said in confidence. You really wouldn't want me to betray you or my peers. Would you?"

Susan Anne Viper's face hardened, and she responded in a tight voice. "Well, I was not asking you to spy on anyone. I just suggested that for the good of the district you share any potential problems with me. But, forget I ever mentioned it. It really isn't important."

With that, Superintendent Viper stood, snapped up her belongings, and departed. Jessica knew she had done the right thing, yet she seriously wondered if she had damaged her own career.

Epilogue: For more than two weeks Superintendent Viper avoided Jessica. She would not return Jessica's calls. At a district-twide function, Susan Anne avoided Jessica's company. Jessica Chang felt the sting from Superintendent Viper's bite. Then, miraculously, the deep freeze ended. Susan Anne appeared at Jessica's door and spoke to her as if nothing had happened. She behaved like her "old self." Neither woman ever broached the spying issue again. Things returned to normal. Jessica Chang worked successfully for Susan Anne Viper for another three years. When Jessica moved on to a new position, Susan Anne gave her a glowing letter of recommendation.

HOW TAXING ARE SUCH ENCOUNTERS?

Your colleagues view such an unethical request as a **4–more stressful** on the one-to-five scale. It is interesting to note that the average rating for administrators with less than five years of experience was a 5. One can only speculate as to the meaning of this finding. Perhaps the most positive interpretation is that novice administrators have less experience in this matter. They are less secure in their attitudes and position. As their personal esteem and position strengthen and solidify, stress in this type of situation decreases. Veterans gave this type of conversation a 3.5 rating. This suggests that they have successfully handled similar encounters and feel more secure in their positions and belief systems. Therefore, with experience, this type of confrontation will become more manageable.

5–most stressful	4–more stressful	3– stressful	2–little stress	1–no stress

A PSYCHOLOGICAL PERSPECTIVE OF THIS SITUATION: WHAT DO WE KNOW ABOUT PEOPLE WHO DO NOT PRACTICE THE SAME CODE OF ETHICS AS MOST PROFESSIONALS?

One wonders how a successful administrator could make such a glaring gaffe. Obviously, Superintendent Viper had her own agenda. She was not thinking of the consequences of her behavior. Rather, she was more interested in how the information would be useful to her and how pliable her new principal was going to be. If she were successful in her manipulation, she was going to mold Jessica into a useful tool who would do her bidding. We can presume she wanted the information to gain greater personal control of her district and her employees. To Superintendent Viper, people were pawns on a chessboard and she was the chess master. No pawn was expected to question her motives or turn down her requests.

Ms. Viper was very self-centered. She was not concerned with the needs of the school district but, rather, with how the school district satisfied her own needs. This was a grandiose position to take, but there are many narcissistic people who take it. Ms. Viper lacked the ability to empathize with others. Ms. Viper, like other narcissistic people, did not care about the reactions of others because she did not have the same feelings as they did (American Psychiatric Association, 1994). Susan Anne Viper had no difficulty in exploiting others because others existed only to satisfy her. She "knew" that her personal worth was far greater than their worth. She believed they should automatically comply with her requests.

Ms. Viper's needs left her vulnerable to miscalculation. She had no doubt that Jessica was going to do her bidding. When Jessica did not respond positively to her suggestion, she acted in an angry and petulant manner because she did not get her way. She was the spoiled child throwing a tantrum. She kept her distance from Jessica for several weeks and then acted as if nothing had happened. Ms. Viper is so self-centered that she could not be bothered by such trifles as a rejection by Jessica. She was more concerned with her next move on the chessboard than with how Jessica responded. Given the opportunity in the future, Superintendent Viper may punish Jessica for her integrity, but she has no time to waste thinking about Jessica's feelings or behavior.

HOW WELL DID THE ADMINISTRATOR HANDLE AN UNETHICAL PROPOSITION?

A Practitioner's View

Jessica Chang should be congratulated. This was a very awkward situation and a potentially very damaging conversation. Being asked to engage in unethical behavior is distasteful. Genuinely seeking to be leaders and role models, most school administrators, like Jessica, would immediately reject such an offer. In today's vernacular, we would tell the person to "kiss off." As Jessica realized, that natural reaction is not easy when you are confronted by the boss. Being approached by one's superordinate adds an enormous amount of stress and danger.

Jessica not only had to remain true to her beliefs and convictions, but she also had to directly oppose Superintendent Viper. Jessica did not naively choose to refuse her superintendent. She made her choice knowing full well the ramifications of her action. Jessica understood that strained relations, ostracizing, negative evaluations, and firing were all real possibilities. Still she acted. Ms. Chang made an ethical choice and was prepared to live with the possible consequences. Principal Jessica Chang demonstrated great courage and moral fortitude.

The current literature is filled with articles extolling the virtues of character development in our curriculum for students. It eloquently urges us to address this element in the development of the pupil's affective domain. Rightfully, the literature puts a great priority on character and moral shaping. C. Anne Lewis (1998) takes this conviction one step further. She insists that students need positive demonstrations of character. Other experts state that students must have examples of positive ethical behavior to successfully internalize these beliefs (Ryan & Bohlin, 1999; Uchida, Cetron, & McKenzie, 1996). In our vignette, Jessica Chang is a shining example for her students, staff, and community. Jessica Chang has character.

Another issue addressed in this sketch is the need to deal with an administrator who is defined by Kaiser (2003) as the Warrior Administrator. Kaiser explains that Warrior Administrators must win at all costs. Normal conventions, ethics, or standards do not bind them. Warriors play by different rules or by no rules at all. Even true educational leaders, like Jessica, find hostile conversations with this type of individual almost impossible to cope with. In disagreements, Warriors win most of the time. Superintendent Viper is a Warrior. Jessica Chang understood that her position was tenuous at best with Superintendent Viper. Yet, she persisted. Jessica stood firm in her convictions. What she did was difficult and dangerous, but ethical. Here, here, Jessica Chang!

A Clinical View

This is one of those situations that we hope will never occur. Jessica was asked to engage in outrageous behavior. She was forced to make a choice between her own set of values and the risk of alienating her boss. If she accepted the boss's "black bag mission," Jessica was agreeing to become a spy. Would this lead to other secret missions?

Put yourself in Jessica's place. If you engage in this behavior, what will the boss really think of you? If you don't accept the mission, you run the risk of alienating your boss and making your position less secure. However, there is not much lost by turning down the superintendent's request. When she asks you to engage in this behavior, the relationship changes. You no longer see her in the same light. You have discomforting knowledge about how she runs her school system.

A second consideration is the changed relationship that will inevitably occur between district administrators. Jessica can no longer speak freely or frankly with her colleagues. She will never know for sure who is already a "Viper Spy."

The whole scenario sounds ludicrous, but it is a story that is based upon fact. In this situation, Jessica's choice was the best one for herself and others. There will inevitably be times when each of us is caught in ridiculous, unbelievable, and ludicrous situations and still must behave professionally and responsibly.

A third point worth discussing is professional standards. Where is our *binding* code of ethics? The professions of medicine, law, and psychology have binding codes of conduct that carry penalties or the revoking of licensure if violated. Yes, in recent times, educators have identified professional standards and expected ethics, dispositions, and behaviors. One example is *The Code of Ethics for School Administrators,* adopted in 1976 by the Executive Board of the American Association of School Administrators. In November 1996, the Council of Chief State School Officers adopted the *Interstate School Leaders Licensure Consortium Standards for School Leaders* (ISLLC Standards), in which Standard 5 is dedicated to ethics. *The California Professional Standards for Educational Leaders* (CPSELS) was adopted by that state in May 2001. Standard 5 of the CPSELS addresses personal and professional ethics. All of the above are excellent examples. However, as educators, we need to consider adopting one standard national code of ethics that, like those of our fellow professionals in other fields, is binding and has "teeth." This action will help individuals understand their role and obligations as educational professionals and provide guidance on a day-to-day basis.

Yes, there are laws that we must follow. However, the purpose of the law may be different from the purpose of a code of ethics. Laws are usually designed to give rights or protect the rights of certain parties, or to define state requirements. By contrast, a code of ethics sets forth standards of behavior for a profession. There may be times when ethical responsibilities conflict with law. In professions where there is a binding code of ethics, and the code and the law conflict, the professional has the responsibility to clarify the nature of the conflict, make known his or her commitment to the ethics code, and, to the extent that it is feasible, seek to resolve the conflict in a way that permits the fullest adherence to the ethics code.

In this scenario, Ms. Viper did request that Jessica Chang violate a professional code of ethics. However, too few practitioners are familiar with our initial developmental strides. Too few educators know where to turn for support. And, unfortunately, there are too many school administrators who, like Viper, would disregard any code unless it carried immediate and strong penalties if violated. So, as of today, Jessica must heavily rely on her own devices. She can take comfort in the fact that her personal and professional code is far superior to her boss's code. Jessica Chang, along with all educators, must eagerly await a more widely disseminated, accepted, intense, and binding code of ethics.

ADDITIONAL SUGGESTIONS: WHAT ELSE COULD AND SHOULD YOU DO IN SIMILAR SITUATIONS?

1. Additional suggestions can be made regarding Principal Chang's behavior. One suggestion to Jessica might be to argue with Susan Anne that to breach a confidence with her peers could backfire. If her colleagues learn of her betrayal, it would render her effectiveness as a resource and support person useless. It would make fellow principals more wary of Susan Anne Viper. Peer knowledge of Jessica's behavior might have a serious negative impact on the district climate. It is conceivable that Superintendent Viper might react positively to these arguments. Yet it is questionable whether such repugnant behavior is worth the effort.

2. Jessica Chang, like all neophyte administrators, must develop positive relations with leading community citizens. This includes school board members, business leaders, active service individuals, and political powerhouses. If a person is held in high esteem by leading citizens, he or she is insulated from unjust attacks. In this case, Jessica will find that she has been inoculated from future viper bites (Kosmoski, 1999a). Be proactive!

IN WHAT OTHER CASES DO THE LEARNED TECHNIQUES APPLY?

As educators, we desperately wish to believe that our constituents are honorable and ethical. Generally, this is true. But they, too, are humans. In any organization, there are unscrupulous, immoral, and unethical individuals. Occasionally, we encounter people who propose unethical actions and conspiracies. Offers can come from many sources—superordinates, peers, subordinates, community members, and, yes, even from students.

Most of us have experienced incidents where a parent demands or pleads for a grade or room change. Teachers have asked us to look the other way as they leave before dismissal. Some of us have been threatened with "bad press" or offered bribes of personal or school-related rewards if we acquiesce to an inappropriate proposal. Some central office administrators regularly must fend off vendors who offer remuneration for district contracts. It would not be exaggerating to suggest that school administrators experience 5 to 10 daily encounters where ethics are called into play.

As educational leaders, we must be committed and ready to act. School administrators have great power and with that power inherently comes great responsibility to act ethically. We must take time to examine and affirm our personal belief systems. We must set personal limits for professional behaviors. What do we value and how will we respond to improper offers? Self-reflection will serve us well. If we are clear about our position and how we will respond prior to being approached, we will be able to act more decisively and satisfactorily. Understand that our personal belief systems extend throughout our personal and professional lives. We become our ethics and our ethics become us.

AN ADDITIONAL CONSIDERATION REGARDING A CODE OF ETHICS

School administrators' actions are shaped by their own personal code of ethics. Actions of effective individuals are most often determined by their belief in righteousness. In *The Healing of America* (1997), Marianne Williamson sadly pointed out that our national conscience barely exists and standards of behavior are blurred. She contends that responsible individuals, like school administrators, must develop their own set of values, or code of ethics. Williamson urges us to rethink our individual values, ethics, and morals.

Believing their members need a standard for which they are accountable, physicians, psychologists, lawyers, and other professional groups have established these codes. They assert that a code of ethics sets a standard that members can accept and to which they can aspire (Levinas, 1985; Mackie, 1990; Williams, 1985). However, after a thorough search of the current literature, no existing code of ethics for the school administrator was found.

As professionals, we, too, could use a standard by which to measure our actions and behaviors. A code of ethics for school administrators is essential. Therefore, we, the authors, have personally developed a rudimentary code based upon the findings obtained from surveys from 150 educators (Kosmoski & Pollack, 1999). The goal was to establish an initial standard for professionals that can be discussed, refined, and revised over time. The product of our efforts is "The School Administrators' Code of Ethics" found in Resource A.

Given this code as a starting point, each of us can develop our own personal code of ethics. After reviewing the standard, we can reflect upon how it matches, coincides, or differs from our existing belief system. Aligning the two into a synthesis by which we can live will result in the establishment of our own professional code of ethics.

SUMMARY

- As administrators, it seems inevitable that we will receive unethical proposals. Expect and be prepared for them. Know your position and what you plan to do prior to such a hostile conversation.

- Understand that confronting and opposing a Warrior superordinate is both dangerous and often unsuccessful. Support from above is one of the few protections from unscrupulous Warrior bosses.
- As educational leaders, we have a genuine responsibility to serve as ethical role models for our students, staff, and community. This is not easy, but necessary. As the proverbial great-aunt Carrie reminds us, "If you can't stand the heat, get out of the kitchen."
- Self-reflection on this topic is a good way to internally clarify your ethical position. It affords us additional strength when tested.

SUGGESTED READINGS

Reviewing Existing Standards for School Administrators

Council of Chief State School Officers. (1996, November). *The Interstate School Leaders Licensure Consortium Standards for School Leaders* (ISLLC Standards). Retrieved June 2004 from www.ccsso.org

State of California. (2001, May). *The California Professional Standards for Educational Leaders* (CPSELS). Retrieved July 2004 from www.acsa .org/doc_files/CPSELS%20card.pdf

Developing Personal Values

Ryan, K., & Bohlin, K. E. (1999). *Building character in schools*. San Francisco: Jossey-Bass.

Williamson, M. (1997). *The healing of America*. New York: Simon & Schuster.

CHAPTER SIX

Combating Charges of Discrimination

THE STORY: An Angry Parent Accuses the Assistant Superintendent of Discrimination

THE PLACE: Washington Middle School in a Major Rust Belt City

D r. Zeke Brock pulled into the school parking lot and stopped his car in the slot marked "District Administrators." He briefly paused and gathered both his thoughts and papers before joining the Washington Middle School Multidisciplinary Team and Ricky Murphy's mother in the conference room. He recalled that it had been several years since he had personally conducted a school-level meeting.

Most concerned, agitated, or skeptical parents were finally agreeable when the district recommended special education services for their child. Even when parents were frightened or upset, they usually could be convinced to cooperate and do what was best for their child. Yet, in his career as assistant superintendent of special education, he had periodically experienced resistant, angry, and hostile parents who fought tooth and nail against accepting help.

The fact that the middle school team had asked him to lead this multidisciplinary conference (MDC) told him that this was not going to be an easy placement. They obviously felt they needed additional support and "clout" from the central office. This was truly unusual. The Washington Special Education Team and their principal were highly competent, seasoned, and thorough, and excellent communicators. Washington was the best they had in the district. Zeke also knew that the state courts had ruled that a student could be placed against the wishes of the parents if a majority at the MDC voted to provide services.

To refresh his memory, Zeke mentally reviewed what he had read in Ricky's permanent school file. Ricky had been in three elementary schools and retained once before coming to Washington. Today, Ricky was a struggling 14-year-old seventh grader. Teacher comments on his report cards indicated that his primary difficulty as far back as kindergarten was with language arts. Records revealed that he was a quiet and shy loner. There was no indication of behavior disorder. At the request of regular classroom teachers, Ricky had been tested in second, fifth, and now again in seventh grade. The results of the test batteries were similar. Each clearly indicated that he was learning disabled and falling farther and farther behind his peers. Today he was reading at the third-grade level and his math scores were at the sixth-grade level. His Full Scale IQ was consistently found to be in the normal range. However, his Performance IQ scores were consistently better than his Verbal IQ scores. Apparently, this was a clear case of a child with a learning disability who needed special help in language arts. Zeke wholeheartedly agreed with the tentative plan of studies prepared jointly by the special education coordinator and the future reading teacher for Ricky. The plan was comprehensive, achievable, and, in his opinion, most appropriate.

Zeke made a mental note that Ricky's single parent, Ms. Mary Lou Murphy, had adamantly refused services for Ricky on two previous occasions. At both meetings, she had exploded, yelled profanities, and made irrational accusations about the team. He also recalled that there were numerous accounts of Ms. Murphy not returning calls or appearing at scheduled meetings. From the social worker's survey, Dr. Brock learned that Mary Lou Murphy was a high school dropout, never married, and the mother of five children—Ricky being the oldest with two elementary-age sisters and twin two-year-old brothers. On a positive note, Zeke reminded himself that there was no evidence or accounts of neglect or abuse in the nine-year history he had studied.

Now, Zeke Brock gathered his briefcase and Ricky's school file. He locked the car door and headed straight toward the school's large conference room. Having read all the documentation and having spoken yesterday directly to Principal Larry Lamont and Valerie Brokowski, Washington's coordinator of special education, Zeke was updated and ready to do his job and get this child the help he needed.

After signing in at the front door, Dr. Brock proceeded directly to the west wing. In the brightly lit corridor where the conference room was located, he saw Larry Lamont waiting. He smiled and waved at exactly the same time Larry acknowledged him.

When they were face to face, Larry said, "Good news and bad news. The good news is that the team is all present and Ms. Murphy is in the building. She went to my office and Mrs. Anderson, my new office clerk, is escorting her here. The bad news is that she brought her twin boys with her and, at two years old, they will be a handful while we are trying to have a serious discussion."

Zeke had an idea, brightened, and replied, "Ask Mrs. Anderson to remain and take the toddlers across the hall to play. Hopefully, Ms. Murphy will understand the difficulty of having the children present and accept our alternative if we pose the suggestion properly."

"Good thinking. We'll try that."

With that said, Larry opened the door and the two of them greeted those assembled. Sitting around the table were Valerie Brokowski; Michael Riordan, projected special education teacher; Judy Homequest, social worker; Stewart Sicolo, school psychologist; Ella May Dennis, Ricky's present homeroom teacher; and Jeremy Osanto, reading specialist. They were quite a heterogeneous group!

Larry Lamont slipped back out to greet the newcomers. Zeke used the time to choose a chair at the narrow portion of the table. This placed him directly opposite and as close as possible to the two remaining seats. When they finally sat down, Zeke would be sitting directly across from Larry and Ms. Murphy.

Shortly, the door opened and there stood Mary Lou Murphy with a child in each arm. She was followed by Larry and Mrs. Anderson. As she clutched the chubby, blonde fraternal twins closer to herself, her eyes darted around the room and then halted directly on Zeke. Mary Lou looked very wary and definitely defiant.

Zeke was neither put off nor intimidated. He smiled broadly and introduced himself.

"Good afternoon, Ms. Murphy. I'm Zeke Brock. I'm the assistant superintendent of special education for the whole district. It's my job to be in charge of providing all the special services needed by our students. Before we begin, I'd like to ask your permission for Mrs. Anderson to take your beautiful boys across the hall where they can play safely and still be nearby. Is that all right with you?"

Still glaring at Zeke, Mary Lou Murphy curtly nodded and then added, "Be sure to leave the door open so I can see them."

"Yes, of course, if you like."

After they all settled in their chairs, Zeke began to make introductions but was summarily and loudly interrupted by Ms. Murphy.

Breathing heavily, she yelled, "Just wait a minute, Mr. Bigshot. I got it. These chickenshits called you in to force me to put my Ricky in a dummy class. I'm not gonna do that no matter what you say."

Visibly shaking and without taking a breath, Mary Lou Murphy continued, "Who the hell do you think you are? You all are picking on us because I have five kids and I'm on welfare. Yes, I live in government housing. It's the only choice I have. I'm responsible. I want to stay home and take good care of my babies. I'm going to keep them safe and not go off to work and leave them with some baby-sitter. They're more important than a couple of extra bucks. I bet you wouldn't do this if I was rich and had the money to sue your ass. Ricky is as smart as any of the other kids. Maybe even smarter than most of 'em. And he's a good boy. So who you trying to kid?"

Her chest heaved and her voice trailed off as she added, "You're just prejudiced! You're only doing this because we're poor. You're picking on me and my kid."

Ms. Mary Lou Murphy folded her arms across her chest, snapped her mouth shut, stuck out her chin, and growled, "Hmm!"

Zeke noticed a tear brimming in the corner of her eye. He felt immediate sympathy for her.

After waiting a good five seconds, Dr. Zeke Brock began in a soft, slow, and low voice.

"Ms. Murphy I can tell you love your son and want to protect him. That's good, but there are three issues I would like you to consider before we make any decisions."

"First, we all agree with you. We believe that Ricky has a good brain. We know this from his intelligence test scores. He's smart but he has been having trouble with reading for a long time. We have *no* wish nor plan to put him in a 'dummy class.' What we need to do is fix this reading problem now before it's too late. All the adults here tell me that Ricky is a very good boy and they all want him to get the best education we can give him. We want him to be successful, graduate from high school, and have a chance for a good life. I know you love him and want that, too."

"Next, we are not prejudiced and we do not discriminate against any of our students. It's not fair to call us prejudiced. Look around this table. I see caring Black, White, and Asian men and women. I see individuals who came from different and, in some cases, tough backgrounds. I see highly educated, trained, and knowledgeable professionals. I don't see prejudiced people who single out or pick on any of our students."

Zeke then grabbed his wallet from his back pocket, pulled out a picture, and slowly slid it across the table to Ms. Murphy.

"Look at that. It's my Grandma Emily, my sister, and me. We're standing in front of our tenement building in the city projects. Grandma raised us after my momma died. We were dirt poor but we loved each other. And here I am today, the 'Big Shot.'"

"You know how I got here, Ms. Murphy? It was Grandma Em. Rest her soul. She always said to us, 'Do what they tell you in school. Learn. Work hard and do your best and you can be anything you want when you grow up.'"

"Finally, I'm here because I do have the last word when it comes to what services we will provide for Ricky. I am convinced that working together with everyone at this table, we can agree on what is best for him and then get it for him. Now, is that okay with you?"

Slowly, Mary Lou Murphy nodded and Zeke Brock finally began an hour-long conference that ended both peacefully and successfully. Ricky would remain in his regular classes with the exception of his rotating one-hour elective class, which would be replaced with a one-on-one intensive reading class. Dr. Brock also made a note to the team that they should try to communicate regularly and often with mom so they could nourish a good working relationship with the home.

HOW TAXING ARE SUCH ENCOUNTERS?

Survey results show that this type of confrontation was considered a **4—more stressful.** School administrators, particularly at the elementary level, reported that they experience more volatile situations dealing with special education placements than performing any other task. Because of the frequency of these occurrences, this type of encounter needs to be examined.

In addition, our colleagues report that accusations of discrimination are becoming more commonplace. Survey data identifies unsupported charges of discrimination as being on the rise and of great concern to our colleagues. Again, this situation was awarded a stress factor score of **4–more stressful**.

5–most stressful	4–more stressful	3– stressful	2–little stress	1–no stress

A PSYCHOLOGICAL PERSPECTIVE OF THIS SITUATION: WHAT PROMPTED THE PARENTAL OUTBURST

Ms. Murphy knows she is right! By being resistant to special education services, she is taking a very strong position. As a mother, she is acting in a fashion that she believes is in the best interest of her child. As a member of a lower socioeconomic class and the mother of a possibly learning disabled child, she knows the frustration of trying to get others to listen to her concerns. Furthermore, she recognizes her lack of power in this meeting. She has been approached at least twice before concerning Ricky and has resisted the overtures from the school district. It seems to her that whenever the school wants something, she must respond, but whenever she wants something, the school does not have to respond. There is nothing wrong with her taking a strong position even though it is harrowing and emotionally draining for all. In desperation, she is tearfully saying, "Show me!"

Ms. Murphy's primary fear is whether this program will really work. And, what will singling out her child do to his self-esteem and social relations with peers? A review of the literature of various reading interventions demonstrates that preventing humiliation and loss of self-esteem for children similar to Ricky is a very "iffy" business with many unanswered concerns and no guarantees (Gersten, Fuchs, & Baker 2001; Mastropieri & Scruggs, 1997). Stand-alone reading programs appear to have less success than those coupled with support services from the school counselor or school psychologist.

The MDC team responds immediately to one of Ms. Murphy's fears by showing her good information to support their position that Ricky needs additional services. They relate to Ms. Murphy that he is doing poorly in the classroom, did poorly on the verbal portion of the intelligence test, and is doing poorly interpersonally. However, they do not address several issues. For example, the scenario doesn't show that Zeke has reviewed Ricky's medical records. Has he had his hearing checked? Does he have a vision problem? Is environment part of their battery for placement?

Ms. Murphy knows that no matter what the team called the change in Ricky's schedule, his peers will identify him as going to a "dummy" class of some type. They, too, must admit that no matter how they couch their words, they *are* singling out Ricky for special treatment and that treatment will be noticed by his peers. Therefore, this team must find a way to turn a potentially negative situation into a positive experience. Services to emotionally support and bolster Ricky during his reading program are key to long-term success. Ricky's Individual Education Plan (IEP) must include the services of the school counselor, school psychologist, or both. The use of these professionals will minimize the emotional risk for Ricky.

HOW WELL DID THE ASSISTANT SUPERINTENDENT OF SPECIAL EDUCATION COMBAT CHARGES OF DISCRIMINATION AND ACCOMPLISH HIS GOAL?

A Practitioner's View

Dr. Zeke Brock did a very professional job in this situation because he did his homework before meeting with Ms. Murphy. He was not baited by her words or physical reactions. He kept the discussion on track in a kind, yet professional, manner. He had a goal to get Ricky the services the boy sorely needed and he was not distracted by verbal fireworks or personal attacks.

Zeke obviously prepared before initiating the meeting. He gathered and reviewed all the available reports and tests results. He made sure there were no new circumstances by speaking with key participants the day prior to the scheduled meeting. Next, Zeke took the time to digest and synthesize the facts to develop a broader understanding of the present situation. Finally, Zeke did what true leaders do: He reflected upon his ultimate goal before jumping into the fray. Zeke clearly knew and was committed to his final objective (services for Ricky) before the encounter. Dr. Brock was not baited into behaving unprofessionally when Ms. Murphy unjustly accused him of being prejudiced. Many educators report that, although the accusation is unfounded, distraught parents have accused them of discriminating because of prejudice. They report that constituents have accused them of gender, racial, and economic discrimination. Unfair? Probably. But it is a fact in our society today. McEwan (2004) points out that in today's schools we must be prepared to deal with parents who are difficult and unpredictable.

It was clear that as an experienced administrator, Zeke Brock was prepared and certainly not shocked by Ms. Murphy's tirade. He appears to have thought this possibility through ahead of time and had his response ready. To anticipate potential problems before they occur is a good leadership practice.

Experts explain that there are two basic types of conflict. There is substantive conflict and there is emotional conflict. Substantive conflict is a difference of opinion over a goal, process, method, topic, fact, or issue. Substantive conflict can be a healthy and valuable tool to reach resolution. However, emotional conflict focuses on personalities and, often, irrational feelings (Kaiser, 2003). Little of value and less positive results occur during emotional conflict, and therefore it should be avoided by the experienced leader. Dr. Brock did a masterful job of keeping this verbal confrontation in the realm of substantive conflict and thereby helped to ensure a positive conclusion.

Finally, Zeke Brock stayed focused and committed throughout this exchange. He knew what he planned to have as a final resolution and was not deterred. Ricky did get the services necessary for him to be successful.

A CLINICAL VIEW

Dr. Brock and the MDC team worked hard to show consideration and deference to Ms. Murphy. They attempted to structure the environment for her convenience. Zeke Brock volunteered some of his own background and shared family values to lessen the distance between her and the committee. Most important, he attempted to respond to her concerns about Ricky. He explained the positives and negatives about Ricky. Zeke affirmed Ms. Murphy's belief that Ricky is at least an average kid, intellectually and emotionally. Zeke specified his limitations so she could consider whether the team was being critical or supportive of her child. Dr. Brock explained how the specialized program would minimize the disruption of Ricky's routine.

A placement decision made between Ms. Murphy and the MDC team is more likely to work when it is consensual rather than when it is imposed. The MDC team need not operate in an autocratic manner. Ms. Murphy's support will go a long way toward overcoming the next hurdle: getting Ricky's cooperation and support for the program.

ADDITIONAL SUGGESTIONS: WHAT ELSE COULD AND SHOULD YOU DO IN SIMILAR SITUATIONS?

1. Resistance to offers of assistance is often an issue of trust. Most seasoned administrators would agree that this form of confrontation is not unusual. Rather, special education placements are often highly emotional situations. Many parents themselves have had bad experiences in school. They question our motives and veracity. We need to establish a bond of trust before we can successfully engage the parent.

2. Another complication is that many parents personalize their child's needs and feel that the schools are blaming them for their child's lack of success. Or they blame themselves and react defensively to overtures of help. They question themselves and ask, "What have we done wrong?" Therefore, a wise administrator must realize that special education placements must skillfully address the child's needs *and* the parents' insecurity and guilt.

3. It is worth mentioning that, in contrast to parents who resist placement, there are parents or guardians who demand

unnecessary placements. Although a student may not qualify for any special assistance, be it remediation or acceleration, there are those adults who demand services. These people cost the sincere administrator valuable time and effort, and cause additional stress. Clear and decisive communications with these individuals and a "heads up" to one's superordinate is recommended.

4. One omission in Dr. Brock's handling of this situation was student contact. It is a good practice to observe and meet with potential special education students before meeting with the parents. Clearly, many of the team members had frequent and lengthy interaction with Ricky prior to the MDC. However, it would have helped Zeke to meet with the student before the MDC. Such a meeting would have provided him with a clearer picture of Ricky and laid the foundation for cooperation and better communication with Ricky's mom.

Some information is best learned by observation and direct contact. How much easier it would have been for Zeke if he could have shared positive impressions of Ricky with Ms. Murphy. For example, if Zeke had spent time with the boy, he might have been able to report to the mom something like, "I know Ricky is quiet, but when he starts talking about his family he gets a great twinkle in his eye" or perhaps he could have said, "He sure knows a lot about baseball." Honest and positive statements such as these can transcend emotional barriers.

IN WHAT OTHER CASES DO THE LEARNED TECHNIQUES APPLY?

Accusations of discrimination or prejudice can come from any quarter. Regardless of their motivation, adversaries in today's society often "pull out the race, gender, or poverty card." Accepting this possibility will help the savvy administrator handle any confrontation where this tactic is attempted. If you, the administrator, have regularly used self-reflection and have concluded that you are not prejudiced toward or against any given group, stand firm. An accusation is not a fact. Believe in yourself and do not be intimidated. Zeke Brock spoke to his own situation. Honest, equivocal, and positive statements that relate directly to one's self should work in most cases.

SUMMARY

- In general, we find accusations of discrimination and prejudice taxing. We also find many formal meetings regarding special education issues stressful encounters. In both of these situations, our colleagues rate the stress level a **4–more stressful.**
- Some strategies that facilitate emotionally charged meetings include preparation prior to the meeting, knowledge of the facts, control of one's response to false accusations, and focus on the meeting's outcome and goal.
- Understand that parents who represent their child at special education (or any other type) meetings often explode and may make unfounded accusations. Furthermore, understand that these parents are often sincere in their response, regardless of whether their manner is appropriate, civil, or even rational. However, there are other parents or constituents who deliberately use accusations of discrimination for shock value in order to gain an advantage in a heated discussion.

SUGGESTED READINGS

Learning How to Deal With Difficult Parents

McEwan, E. K. (2004). *How to deal with parents who are angry, afraid, or just plain crazy* (2nd ed.). Thousand Oaks, CA: Corwin.

Keeping Abreast of Social Issues in Our Schools

Brantlinger, E. (1991). Social class distinctions in adolescents' reports of problems and punishment in school. *Behavioral Disorders, 17,* 36–46.

Turnbull, A. P., Shank, M., Turnbull, R., & Smith, S. J. (2003). *Exceptional lives: Special education in today's schools.* New York: Prentice Hall.

Understanding the Gravity and Personal, Physical, and Emotional Effects of Highly Charged Confrontations

Kosmoski, G. J., Pollack, D. R., & Schmidt, L. J. (1999). Jekyll or Hyde: Changes in leadership styles and the personalities of beginning school administrators. *Illinois Schools Journal, 79*(1), 23–34.

Suinn, R. M. (2001). The terrible twos: Anger and anxiety hazardous to your health. *American Psychology, 56*(1), 27–36.

Understanding the Challenge of a Career in School Administration

Gates, S. M., Ringel, J. S., Santibanez, L., Chung, C. H., & Ross, K. (2003). *Who is leading our schools? An overview of school administrators and their careers.* New York: Rand.

Understanding the Challenges of NCLB

Ambrosio, J. (2004). No Child Left Behind: The case of Roosevelt High School. *Phi Delta Kappan, 85*(9), 709–712.

CHAPTER SEVEN

Discouraging the Dependent Personality

THE STORY: Go Right Ahead, Miss Butler

THE PLACE: City Neighborhood High School

T om Brite felt very good this afternoon. As he sauntered to the media center, Tom mentally rehearsed his remarks for this evening. He was being honored as the "Person of the Month" by the Young Afro-American Professionals Guild. This was surely very good for his career.

Tom marveled at his good fortune. In the last five years, life had moved very fast and had been very good to him. Still in his twenties, Tom had left the classroom to become a dean. He had married, earned his administrator's license, and been promoted to assistant principal.

Tom looked up as he turned the corner to see Emily Butler standing at the entrance to the media center. It was too late to turn around or duck into an empty classroom. Miss Butler had already seen him. She was smiling and waving to him.

As Tom neared, Emily spoke. "Good afternoon, Mr. Brite. I've been looking for you. I really need your help."

"Of course! What can I do for you?" replied Tom.

Eagerly, Miss Butler continued, "Do you remember when I asked you if it would be all right to send a letter home to my students' parents, urging them to attend Open House? Well, since you felt it was a good idea, I went ahead and wrote a draft. I hope it's okay."

"I'm sure it's just fine," said Tom.

Emily Butler rushed on, "Well, I don't want to take any chances. Will you please look it over? Just make any corrections or suggestions right on this copy and put it in my box. I'd really appreciate it."

"I guess I can do that," muttered Tom.

"Great!" exclaimed Emily as she flashed him a huge smile.

She shoved the letter into Tom's hand and headed down the hall. Almost as an afterthought, Emily Butler turned and said, "Well, thanks again, Mr. Brite. Could you make sure it's in my mail-box by the end of the day?" With that parting remark, she was gone.

He watched her leave. Tom couldn't believe it. Emily Butler had done it again. Somehow, she had him doing her job. She always seemed so helpless and needy, but here he was doing her dirty work.

Thinking back over the last few weeks, Tom could remember her asking his help, permission, or advice maybe four or five times. But then, Emily Butler was always asking for something.

Tom just didn't understand it. Emily Butler had been a teacher at this high school for close to 30 years. Why, she was older than his mother. Emily Butler was a veteran, competent, and caring teacher. Maybe a little set in her ways, but one of the school's best. Emily Butler was an institution. Tom Brite shook his head sadly. Why couldn't she make her own decisions and act like a professional? Why couldn't she just leave him alone?

HOW TAXING ARE SUCH ENCOUNTERS?

All the administrators surveyed admitted that they have had to deal with a Miss Butler in one form or another. These nondecisive and dependent individuals exist in most schools. Administrators felt that dealing with the ever-present Miss Butler was a constant irritation. Many felt this type of person should be tolerated, endured, and appeased because little could be done to rectify the situation.

They rated this type of confrontation as a **3–stressful** and somewhat taxing. However, because there are so many Miss Butlers to contend with in our schools, this situation is worth exploring. The damaging effects of stress are increased not only by the intensity (quality) of an encounter but also by the frequency (quantity) of the event. Debilitating effects of stress are cumulative. If we can decrease this type of frustrating encounter, we can eliminate, or at the very least reduce, our irritation and stress level. Administrators must develop attitudes and practices that can be applied to this kind of subordinate.

5–most stressful	4–more stressful	3– stressful	2–little stress	1–no stress

A PSYCHOLOGICAL PERSPECTIVE OF THIS SITUATION: WHAT DO WE KNOW ABOUT DEPENDENT PERSONALITY?

In psychology, we talk about personality or the general psychological makeup of the individual. We also use the term *personality* when we want to talk about long-standing patterns of behavior. The *Diagnostic and Statistical Manual-IV (DSM-IV)* (American Psychiatric Association, 1994) describes behaviors that are pathological. Pathological behaviors are seen as deleterious to self or others. Personality disorders are patterns of behavior that typically begin in childhood and are very resistant to change. Miss Butler is an institution. She has been with the school system for 30 years. If she truly has a dependent personality, then she has engaged in this behavior with previous principals, colleagues, and secretaries. Mr. Brite should query his staff about how much of Miss Butler's work they have been doing. Also, does she take credit for the work her colleagues do for her? If possible, Tom should talk to the previous administrators to find out whether they had the same problem with Emily Butler. Clearly, Miss Butler's problem is not debilitating to her and probably not great enough to be diagnostic. However, her behavior is very inconvenient and unfair to the rest of the staff.

Mr. Brite must discuss Miss Butler's behavior with her. When he does, it is not likely that she will change. Since she has no insight into her own behavior, Tom can expect that his criticism will be very upsetting to her. If this private discussion fails, he could hold a staff meeting in which doing others' work is on the agenda. The purpose should be to focus on the issue of "dependency behaviors" and the expectation that each staff member should complete his or her own work and should not be expected to do the work of others. Tom should not name names nor allow the meeting to become personal or critical of individuals. Rather, the meeting should clearly notify the group that Tom expects a change in behavior. This will affect Emily Butler. Unfortunately, dependent people *always* try to find someone else to take care of them. Tom's meeting might protect the staff from Miss Butler.

HOW WELL DID THE ASSISTANT PRINCIPAL HANDLE THE DEPENDENT TEACHER?

A Practitioner's View

Tom Brite's treatment of Miss Butler is not unusual. Many school administrators placate the needy teacher. At first glance, this approach seems expedient and less stressful for all. Some school administrators would reply, "Why rock the boat?" or "Don't fix it if it ain't broke."

However, a more serious investigation makes us question this approach. Tom's actions did nothing to discourage Miss Butler from continuing to lean upon him or others. If anything, Tom Brite's acquiescence encourages Miss Butler to continue or even escalate her requests for help and attention. This is unfair to him, to Miss Butler, and to all staff members.

This problem will not go away either as a result of ignoring it or complying to avoid causing trouble. If Tom truly wishes to change the situation for himself and his staff, action is required. Put succinctly, Tom handled this ongoing problem poorly.

As the assistant principal, Tom Brite has certain responsibilities to Emily Butler. Research clearly demonstrates that effective educational leaders encourage and guide individual faculty members to grow and become independent thinkers. They encourage risk taking, empowerment, and professionalism (Byham, 1992; Kosmoski & Pollack, 1997; Martinez, 2004). Mr. Brite should keep this directive in mind during any further confrontation with Miss Butler. He should ask himself if his responses to her encourage independent thinking, self-control, and empowerment.

Another strategy that Tom could use is candid discussion. Miss Butler deserves to hear directly from her superordinate any complaints about her behavior. She might not like hearing negatives, but she has the right to know. Tom should arrange for a private meeting with Emily Butler. He should explain his position, using examples of actual events. Points he should include in the meeting are his faith in her ability and professionalism, concerns about her fears and independence, observations, and high expectations of behaviors for all. Even if Tom conducts this meeting with tact and candor, Miss Butler's initial reaction could be negative. However, since she is a competent and successful 30-year veteran, it is quite possible that she might reassess and rethink her behavior.

The research suggests that truly effective educational leaders should operate as often as possible in a collegial style that encourages team effort. That fact would then imply that Tom should indeed relish the opportunity to work with Miss Butler on her parent letter. However, that is not the case in this scenario. These are not usual circumstances. Rather, the story clearly shows that asking Tom for help is just one incident in a long string of behaviors that rob Miss Butler of her independence, professional competence, and task ownership. The particular encounter is not the issue; rather, it is Emily Butler's pattern of behavior. Tom would be wise to judiciously use some laissez-faire tactics with Miss Butler. Sometimes, doing nothing yourself, while encouraging and praising your subordinates, has positive results. For example, Tom could have responded to Miss Butler's request for proofing and editing by saying, "It's not necessary for me to check your work, Miss Butler. I know you are very competent and a true professional. Your letter will be excellent. I trust you to send it out when you're satisfied with its contents." Although a laissez-faire approach should only be used sparingly, there are those rare occasions that merit this style.

Finally, Tom should be concerned about his entire staff. How he relates and responds to Miss Butler's demands has a direct bearing on the school climate. By allowing her to shirk her duties or impose upon others, Mr. Brite gives the impression that poor performance and low expectations are acceptable. Why should other individuals accept leadership positions and behave in a professional, independent manner if Emily Butler is exempt? Tom Brite must accept the responsibility as role model while dealing with individual faculty members (Chase, 1998; Lambert, 1998).

A Clinical View

Dependent people can be very friendly and ingratiating. They will ask for your advice. Then they will ask for your time. Then they will ask for more of your time. Then they will ask for more of your advice. This pattern tends to be very subtle. It may start with a casual question in the hallway. It quickly moves to a visit to your office. It escalates to a phone call at home. On the surface, the questions may seem fair and reasonable. You may not notice that the amount of time taken to answer questions becomes greater and greater. The purpose of visits or calls may appear to be work related but the real purpose is the attention that the dependent person receives from you. You should not see this as a compliment. It simply means that you are more easily manipulated and more gullible than other people. When, not if, this happens, you should simply recognize that your need to do a good job and be open to your subordinates makes you vulnerable to manipulation. If you allow yourself to be manipulated, you reinforce the very behavior that becomes abhorrent to you. You will find that the "demands" placed upon you make it more and more difficult for you to complete your own work.

Although you are not trained as a psychologist, there is a basic strategy that psychologists use when dealing with a dependent personality that will be beneficial to you. First, establish a verbal contract between the person and you. Place limits on the individual. Clarify the individual's and your responsibilities in the work relationship. Hold firm to the agreed-upon contract. If, after the contract is established, a crisis occurs where the dependent person places an inappropriate demand upon you, you must respond. The person is using the demand to measure whether you "care" about him or her. They are testing you and the limits of the relationship. If you go beyond the limits, it is a clear, but unspoken, understanding that you are not in charge.

This is what occurred between Mr. Brite and Miss Butler. He was a new assistant principal who wanted to succeed and form a good working relationship with his staff. Emily Butler found his openness, availability, and caring desirable. She viewed her visits and granted requests as a measure of Tom's caring. He needed to set limits and expectations for Miss Butler and himself. A healthy individual will respond positively to these limits and expectations because they would more clearly define the relationship. However, in Miss Butler's case, she is more likely to feel rejected and perhaps angry when the limits are finally set. Regardless, if Tom Brite follows this suggested course of action, he can be assured that he acted in a professional, appropriate, and caring manner. There is simply nothing more he can do for Emily Butler, short of a referral for counseling. He would have done his best.

Again, the practitioner's and the clinical view of this case vary somewhat, but both provide useful tools and strategies when dealing with dependent or smothering individuals. Take the best of both for future encounters.

ADDITIONAL SUGGESTIONS: WHAT ELSE COULD AND SHOULD YOU DO IN SIMILAR SITUATIONS?

1. Most encounters of this nature are not so severe as to become debilitating, but there are those cases where a dependent person can seriously impede the educational and instructional program. In these incidents, our colleagues suggest stronger measures. They urge you to become proactive, rather than reactive. Tailor your leadership style to match the needs of the dependent individual (Glickman, 1990; Kaiser, 2003). Consider temporarily adopting a directive or authoritarian leadership style. Directly tell, not ask, the dependent person to cease and desist. Spell out your expectations for independent action and your guarantee for support of risk taking.

2. If your district has an Employee Wellness Benefit Program, where counseling is available at no cost, share that

information with the person in question. It is quite possible that the exhibited school behavior is also manifested in the individual's personal life. Maybe counseling is an appropriate and desirable solution.

3. One technique an administrator might use to determine if a subordinate's requests are appropriate or inappropriate is to ask oneself, "Whose problem or job is this?" If the answer is clearly the subordinate, then the administrator should treat the situation as a true dependency problem.

4. Finally, whatever steps you choose to employ with dependent subordinates, remember to do your homework. Because of fairness and accuracy issues as well as contractual and legal considerations, always document inappropriate incidents. Even if it is a simple question in the hall or a distraught call to your home at night, log the event. Perhaps you will never need to use the record, but if you do, you will be prepared.

IN WHAT OTHER CASES DO THE LEARNED TECHNIQUES APPLY?

In both sections, A Practitioner's View and A Clinical View, several suggested actions were given that would apply to a myriad of circumstances. Use a more direct style when working with most beginning teachers and "teacher dropouts." In both cases, the individuals need more direction and structure to be most productive (Glickman, 1990; Kosmoski & Pollack, 1997).

A laissez-faire tactic can be used successfully when two or more staff members are engaged in conflict. In these cases, it is most useful to remain nonjudgmental and allow the parties to resolve the matter themselves. This does not imply disinterest or abandonment, but rather serves as a concerted effort to avoid superimposing your position upon them. The same is true for the dependent person. Refusing to step in can help rather than hinder.

Finally, the practice of documentation applies to most cases you will ever encounter. Accurate record keeping is necessary for the school administrator's effectiveness and, yes, survival.

SUMMARY

- Dependent subordinates can be charming. However, they are manipulating you and others. This is unfair to all—including the dependent person.
- Protect yourself. Continuous encounters with such people can be very draining. Stress is cumulative and can be physically damaging to you. Decrease the number of incidents that cause you undue stress.
- You have a responsibility to discourage this type of behavior. Left unchecked, these actions can be detrimental to the climate and educational program of the school. This type of behavior is detrimental to the cohesiveness and effectiveness of the group—the school community (Cragan & Wright, 1995). Accommodating the needs of dependent individuals helps no one.
- Some techniques you can utilize when dealing with dependent staff members include changing your leadership style to be more direct, adopting some laissez-faire tactics, initiating direct or indirect discussion of the problem, and documenting such decisions.
- In extreme cases, rely on support services.

SUGGESTED READINGS

Increasing Teacher Confidence, Independence, and Empowerment

Byham, W. (with Cox, J., & Harper, K.). (1992). *Zapp! In education.* New York: Fawcett Columbine.

Goodlad, J. I. (1984). *A place called school.* New York: McGraw-Hill.

Lambert, L. (1998). How to build leadership capacity. *Educational Leadership, 55(7)*, 17–19.

CHAPTER EIGHT

Serving as Mediator When Friction Exists

THE STORY: Dick, Jane, and Sally

THE PLACE: A Neighborhood Primary Elementary School

S ally Stalinsky could feel the chill in the air as she entered the usually cheerful conference room. Mrs. Jane Ginn, president of the school's PTO, was studying a notepad in front of her while stroking a calico kitten perched on her left knee. Jane was ignoring Dick Spot, who sat directly opposite her at the round table. Dick was the school's P.E. teacher and, along with Jane, this year's cochair of the annual school picnic. A normally energetic and animated man, Dick seemed edgy and sullen. He even avoided Sally's eyes as she greeted the pair.

This reaction startled Sally. During her four years as principal of Orchard Park Elementary, she had never seen this kind of behavior from either party. Both were easygoing, friendly, and cooperative people. Yes, she knew these two people were having some difficulty finalizing the plans for the upcoming event, but their demeanor was more negative than she had expected.

Jane Ginn had been the one to call her. Jane asked her to intercede with Dick, who was representing the building staff. Jane was so frustrated that she exclaimed, "The PTO has decided not to cosponsor the annual school picnic because of all the changes the teachers are demanding." Even after this outburst, Sally believed that what she had on her hands was simply a lack of communication. She had insisted that the three of them needed to meet to resolve any differences they might be experiencing.

Later, when Sally spoke with Dick, she learned the teachers were very concerned about the way the picnic had been run in the past and that they insisted upon change or the removal of this event from the school calendar. Still, Sally believed resolving the problem was not a big deal. She believed that by facilitating a calm, sincere meeting, she could quickly set things right.

Now, reading Dick and Jane's body language, Sally began to reassess the gravity of the situation. She realized she would need to walk a fine line as peacemaker.

Sally turned to Jane and said, "That's a darling kitten. Is he a new member of the family?" Jane gave her a tight smile and replied, "Thanks. We've had him for two weeks. The children love him. I'm taking him to the vet for shots right after this meeting." Jane seemed to loosen up after speaking.

Next, Sally turned to Dick. "Thanks for coming in during your plan time. Your flexibility about scheduling this meeting certainly helps both Jane and me." Dick only nodded as Sally took a seat between them.

Sally got right to the point. She addressed Dick, "I understand some of the faculty are dissatisfied with the plans for the school picnic."

"Not just some, most don't like the way it's been done in the past. They want me to get it changed or to have it dropped," Dick snorted.

Jane impatiently piped up. "That's nuts! We've done it the same way since my kids started school here 10 years ago. Everybody, I mean the parents and kids, like it just the way it is. Mrs. Stalinsky, you have to make the teachers understand this is really important to all of us. Don't spoil a good thing. The changes the teachers want will really stop a lot of the fun. The PTO has been really good to the school and the teachers. Think about all the support and the funds we have supplied to the school. It's about time the teachers did something we want. Mrs. Stalinsky, you're the principal. Make them back off!"

"Hold on, both of you. There are some critical things here I don't understand. Dick, exactly what changes are the teachers proposing? And why?" queried Sally.

Dick shook his head and made an effort to control his voice. "Mrs. Stalinsky, I explained to Jane that the teachers have three major complaints that must be fixed or we can't support a picnic on school time. First, this is not 10 years ago. Today there are so many working parents that about half of the students don't have a parent who shows up. Those kids feel bad and left out. Mommy or Daddy doesn't bring them 'Mickey D's' or some other special lunch, like the lucky ones. What are we supposed to do with them? Second, this thing lasts an hour and a half. That's too long to keep little children busy. Third, it gets very confusing as to who is responsible for each child. Is the teacher in charge? Or, since the parent is there, is the parent the boss? No one is sure. Someone is going to wander off or get badly hurt. Then what? It's not safe!"

Dick's voice began to speed up and get louder. He was obviously upset with the whole proceeding. However, he continued, "And finally, there are no provisions for the teacher's own lunch. By law, we are entitled to a half hour, duty-free lunch. The teachers feel they need lunch and are entitled to it."

Jane exploded, "Right! You care so little about your students that you wouldn't give up your lunch break once during the school year. Whatever happened to dedication?"

Sally couldn't believe her ears. She was appalled. These usually caring adults were behaving like little elementary schoolchildren themselves. There was no reason for this kind of petty and foolish bickering. Sally thought fast and came up with a temporary solution for each concern. If they couldn't resolve their differences, she would do it for them.

Sally turned to Dick and Jane and calmly said, "Wait a minute. We need to calm down. These are serious concerns, but I believe I have a decent solution for each. See what you think. First, the problem of a special lunch for every child is something we should address. Every student should have a good time. The picnic is supposed to be a reward for a year of hard work. This is our purpose for the picnic. Right? The answer is easy. I'll just have the cafeteria make a picnic lunch, probably something like hot dogs and ice cream. We'll provide lunch for every child and every parent. No one brings lunch from home unless there are special circumstances. I'll need input about the menu. Okay?"

After they grudgingly nodded agreement, Sally continued, "The question of time frame is more serious. Ninety minutes is a long time for little children to be safely supervised. Who is responsible for safety is a good question. Parents are actually guests and the teachers are responsible for the safety of all children while they are on this campus. We need to plan some activities that teachers and parents can monitor for that period of time or we need to shorten the time, so the students are safe. I'll be glad to help you prepare a timetable."

"Now, the last problem is the teachers' lunch period," Sally said. "Dick, this is an internal problem. I'll have to work out a schedule. I only wish you would have come directly to me with this and not troubled Jane. We can and will rectify this."

Dick looked embarrassed but said nothing.

Not seeming to notice, Sally continued, "Now let's check our calendars and see when we can meet again to plan the event timetable. I'm considering something like organized games for part of the time." Jane and Dick remained silent.

After they set their calendars, they all stood up to leave. Neither Dick nor Jane seemed particularly pleased. Well, it was just too bad, Sally thought. She had other things to get done today.

Without forethought, Sally reached over and stroked the kitten's head. "What's his name, Jane?" she asked.

Jane replied, "The children can't agree on a good name."

At that Dick chuckled and quipped, "I'll bet if we put our heads together we can find the perfect name. Remember, we are Dick, Jane, and Sally."

HOW TAXING ARE SUCH ENCOUNTERS?

The administrators who responded to this question felt that acting as a mediator was not particularly stressful. The average rating they gave to this type of situation was a **3–stressful.** However, without exception, all 250 school administrators confirmed that they have served in this capacity with varying degrees of success. They also indicated that properly grappling with this type of situation is essential for the effective practitioner. Interviewed participants believed developing skills as a facilitator or mediator was necessary to become a successful school administrator.

5–most stressful	4–more stressful	3– stressful	2–little stress	1–no stress

A PSYCHOLOGICAL PERSPECTIVE OF THIS SITUATION: WHAT DO WE KNOW ABOUT MEDIATION WHEN PEOPLE ARE IN CONFLICT?

There are times when we are tired, worn out, and have tried to do too much or simply have too much to do. Let's posit that this is the case with Sally. Furthermore, others see her as respectful, warm, friendly, and open. Her style is democratic when it is possible. For this reason, Dick and Jane have come to her together with their problems, seeking an equitable and satisfying resolution of their conflict. When we read this scenario, we see that Sally has acted in a manner that is different from the expectations of Jane and Dick. In this case she has acted by decree. She has placated one and avoided the other. She has placated the PTO president and dismissed for now the concerns of the teachers. Although she advocates a democratic approach, she has acted in an autocratic manner.

Sally failed to fulfill Dick and Jane's need to express themselves. As educators, we find interesting the excuses that students present. For college students who miss a test, there is the "I was sick" excuse, the "My grandmother died" excuse, the "I overslept" excuse, ad infinitum. The excuse is frequently a creative and artistic work that has taken a great deal of time and emotional involvement to prepare. But, what if the teacher changed the ground rules and said, "If you miss a test, it is not necessary to make an excuse. Contact me for an appropriate makeup test time." Many students would have difficulty with this statement. They still would arrive at the office with their well-crafted excuse. When they began their excuse, they would be stopped and told, "That you said you couldn't make it to the test is all I need to know. Let's schedule the makeup test." This would be very disturbing. Students would experience a need to present the excuse. They would try. They would be stopped. They would be frustrated. They would need to talk about their excuse.

Dick and Jane needed to talk. They were very emotionally involved in their issues. Sally created greater difficulties for herself by preventing Dick and Jane from expressing their emotions. She had created a democratic environment, yet acted by decree. Dick and Jane's expectations were not only unmet, they were harshly rebuffed. As a result of her actions, Sally now will have to deal with the conflict she created and will have to give Dick and Jane the opportunity to meet with her. She will need to provide a "Let's sit down and talk" meeting.

HOW WELL DID SALLY CONTEND WITH THE TASK OF MEDIATION?

A Practitioner's View

At best, Sally Stalinsky did a less than average job as the mediator between Dick and Jane. That is not to say that she did not do anything well. She demonstrated a number of positive actions. Unfortunately, the negatives outweighed the positives.

One thing Sally did well was to arrange a meeting with the combatants for the purpose of resolving their differences. She realized that sitting down face-to-face was more effective than speaking privately to each. Her choice of a small conference room with a round table was good. A quiet, safe, and private setting facilitates a free exchange of ideas. Sally also used several techniques to establish a more positive climate at the outset of the meeting. She attempted to create a more cheerful tone by being cordial, friendly, and gracious. Principal Stalinsky was able to identify the key elements of the disagreement. She remained calm while she used appropriate statements that helped to defuse and temper some hostile comments. Finally, the solutions Sally provided were both sensible and feasible.

By contrast, Sally made three blatant and damaging mistakes that merit discussion. First, she misjudged the importance of this encounter. Sally did not recognize the necessity of settling this conflict to the satisfaction of both the PTO president and the faculty representative. Their response to the process and the outcome will affect both internal and external school politics. Dick Spot's report to his constituents could influence the type of community, the level of staff trust, and the building climate. If Dick believes that Sally truly supports the faculty and respects the teachers' position, Orchard Park will have a positive, trusting, and satisfied staff (Hodges, 2004; Martinez, 2004; Pellicer, 2004). Conversely, if Dick feels humiliated, betrayed, undermined, and abandoned, the building atmosphere could shift to the negative.

Sally forgot many basic behaviors that convey sensitivity. She did not heed the powerful advice of Daniel Goleman (1998), who wrote:

> Be sensitive. This is a call for empathy, for being attuned to the impact of what you say and how you say it on the person at the receiving end. Managers who have little empathy . . . are most prone to giving feedback in a hurtful fashion, such as the withering put-down. The net effect of such criticism is destructive: instead of opening the way for a corrective, it creates an emotional backlash of resentment, bitterness, defensiveness, and distance. (p. 154)

We know from the vignette that, prior to the meeting, this elementary school enjoyed a very positive relationship with the PTO. It seems obvious that Jane's feelings about the negotiations and solutions could dramatically affect this relationship, and cooperation between the school and this parent organization. Sally needed to expend more thought and energy when addressing the negotiations between these vital members of the school community. She needed to take this confrontation seriously. Sally was wrong. This was a big deal!

Parent involvement is essential for quality schools. Cavarretta (1998) reminds us that parents should be the school's best friends. Engaged parents do make a measurable positive contribution to the academic success of students. Children excel when their parents are engaged in school activities (Child, 1998; Finn, 1998). Sally had a duty to make her school a place where parents feel comfortable and valuable (Chambers, 1998; Hansen & Childs, 1998).

Next, Sally's attitude, style, and philosophy were clearly bureaucratic, direct, and authoritarian (Kaiser, 2003; Kosmoski & Pollack,

1997; Oliva, 1993). Repeatedly, she told rather than asked. She dictated rather than requested. Instead of helping Jane and Dick identify the points of contention and mutually accept a satisfactory resolution, Sally imposed her interpretation and remedy.

The research from the past decade unequivocally demonstrates that individuals respond more favorably to a democratic, indirect, or pluralistic approach. Statistical results confirm that this philosophy and style have many positive and lasting results (Acheson & Gall, 1992; Glanz & Neville, 1997; Sergiovanni & Starratt, 1988). The interests and well-being of Orchard Park Elementary would have been better served had Sally understood and exercised the principles of a democratic or collegial leadership style.

Finally, Sally Stalinsky exhibited an enormous amount of impatience. Throughout this scenario, she seemed to be in a rush to complete the task. Mediation and consensus building are not tasks but, rather, they are processes. The literature clearly establishes that processes take both patience and time, but are statistically more successful (Martin, 1995; Piper, 1974).

A Clinical View

Jane and Dick are stuck with their emotions concerning their personal issues, and now have the added effect of dashed expectations. Furthermore, Dick may have feelings about being scolded in front of the PTO president. Neither consequence is devastating from a clinical point of view. There is disappointment with Sally. Dick is going to have to report to his fellow teachers that she did not respond to their concerns. One would expect that as soon as Dick and Jane left her office, Sally would realize that she had not managed this meeting to the best of her ability. Would it have been better to try to muster the energy to engage them in a democratic discussion? Probably. Even with the knowledge that a democratic approach is very demanding, Sally should have listened to all sides while maintaining *openness* in the heated discussion. Only then should she have responded. It is much easier to rule by edict, and this is the option that Sally took. However, by choosing to leave issues unresolved, Sally created still more issues and additional work for herself.

Sally must now schedule three meetings to correct the mistakes she made in the original meeting. First, she must schedule a follow-up meeting to work out the picnic details of her decree. Second, she needs to meet with Dick. An apology is in order for scolding him, and particularly in public. Sally needs to listen to his concerns and discuss them one by one. This meeting will most likely need to address the immediate concerns expressed by Dick and also the teachers' relationship with her. A third meeting must be set with Jane. Dick was correct when he indicated that just because an approach was used in the past does not mean that the same approach should be used today. The responsibilities of teachers and administrators are in a constant state of flux as new laws are passed, court decisions are reversed, or requirements are changed by the school board. Sally needs to explain the existing safety and legal concerns to Jane. She needs to help Jane understand what can be allowed and what must be changed. Through open and lengthy discussion, the issues can be resolved. However, if left to fester, the issues will cause pain and suffering for Sally.

ADDITIONAL SUGGESTIONS: WHAT ELSE COULD AND SHOULD YOU DO IN SIMILAR SITUATIONS?

1. Mediation and consensus building between two or more individuals are vital processes that require the school administrator to develop many skills and attributes. Some of these are
   - Communication skills. Individuals with this attribute are clear, precise, courteous, and expressive. They emphasize and reiterate where appropriate.
   - Interpersonal skills. Effective administrators value others and relate well to all.
   - Active listening skills. For specific behaviors, refer to Chapter 1, "Defusing the Angry Screamer."
   - Personal qualities. Effective administrators are patient, empathic, and tolerant, and have a sense of humor.
   - Expertise. The school administrator is knowledgeable and practiced in the principles and paradigms of educational administration.

2. It is virtually impossible to mediate a disagreement where all parties feel they are satisfied with the outcome and feel an ownership for the final decision unless you ascribe to the principles of democratic leadership. Those administrators who use a bureaucratic or direct style would find shared decision making impossible.

IN WHAT OTHER CASES DO THE LEARNED TECHNIQUES APPLY?

Using a collegial approach to mediation can work in every case where there is a difference of opinion. This applies to conflicts between students, staff, and community members (Johnson & Johnson, 1997). Since we know mediation conducted in an indirect or collegial style is more successful and long lasting, it becomes imperative that we adopt this style (Dixon, 1994; Johnson & Johnson, 1991, 1997). The linchpin for success appears to be the mindset that you, the mediator, possess as you serve as facilitator. The opposing parties resolve the dispute with your help. The outcome is not your solution but, rather, it is theirs.

SUMMARY

- Although serving as a mediator is not a particularly stressful experience, it is a duty that all administrators face. The successful conclusion of such confrontations often has grave and far-reaching effects. Therefore, practicing school administrators recognize the importance of this task. This suggests that you constantly need to hone your mediation skills to become an educational leader.
- Some negative practices to avoid while mediating are considering the task as insignificant, becoming impatient or emotionally involved, and forcing your solutions upon the individuals in conflict.
- Some of the positive practices to employ when acting as a mediator include providing a safe, quiet, and private location that promotes a free exchange of ideas; remaining

professional and in control of your own feelings; using communication, listening, and interpersonal skills; identifying the points of disagreement and helping the opposing parties to reach mutually satisfying solutions for each; recognizing the importance of the process as well as the outcome; giving the task sufficient time and patience; and holding true to a collegial or democratic style.

SUGGESTED READINGS

Chambers, L. (1998). How customer-friendly is your school? *Educational Leadership, 56*(2), 33–35.

Goleman, D. (1995). *Emotional intelligence.* New York: Bantam.

Hansen, J. M., & Childs, J. (1998). Creating a school where people like to be. *Educational Leadership, 56*(1), 14–17.

Johnson, D. W., & Johnson, R. T. (1997). Conflict resolution and peer mediation in elementary and secondary schools: A review of the research. *Review of Educational Research, 66*(4), 459–506.

Martin, J. R. (1995). A philosophy of education for the year 2000. *Phi Delta Kappan, 76*(5), 355–359.

Pellicer, L. O. (2004). *Caring enough to lead: How reflective thought leads to moral leadership* (2nd ed.). Thousand Oaks, CA: Corwin Press.

CHAPTER NINE

Disabling the Backstabber

THE STORY: Adiós, Mary! Adiós, Oscar!

THE PLACE: District Office of an Affluent Suburb in the Northwest

O scar Franks hung up the phone and turned to look out of his window. He realized he was still shaking and his heart was pounding. Mrs. Black, school board president, had just given him a brutal tongue-lashing. She wanted both an explanation and an apology for his failure to return her call, which caused her to miss a chance for some wonderful publicity. Oscar knew that Mrs. Black didn't believe the truth when he said he had never received her message, and that if he had, he would have immediately returned her call.

Mrs. Black's parting comments made it very clear that this incident caused him grave professional damage. "Well, it's too late now. I'll just be sure to call the superintendent directly the next time. He knows how to use a phone. Goodbye, Mr. Franks."

Oscar was furious. Mary Bitterman, his secretary, had done it to him again. How many times in the last 10 months had Mary's words or actions made him look foolish, incompetent, and unprofessional? Mary had not only stabbed him in the back, but also turned the knife and watched him bleed. Earlier this week, one of the principals who stopped by mentioned that Mary's coldness and unfriendliness bordered on rudeness. Yesterday, Bill Rolinsky joked that his secretary admitted that "Mary the Back-stabber" had roasted Oscar to well done at the monthly secretaries' card party. Finally, this morning he had to redo three of the five purchase orders she had typed. Now this! How much more was he supposed to take?

It was no accident that Mrs. Black's message to call her immediately was lost. Oscar was sure Mary would have some excuse, plausible or otherwise. He also was sure that Mary Bitterman had deliberately set him up. For the 10 months Oscar had been stuck with her, it had been a nightmare. He couldn't believe how much she was able to hurt him. He only knew she could.

Oscar shook his head as he recounted the events that led up to today. It all began quite innocently. Superintendent Larry Hatcher had asked Oscar to do a personal favor for him. Larry was not only Oscar's boss but also his good friend. Oscar had enjoyed working for Larry during his six years as assistant superintendent of pupil/personnel services. Oscar was glad to do his boss a favor.

Since Oscar's secretary was finally retiring, Larry asked Oscar to give Mary Bitterman a try. He explained that Mary wanted to transfer to the central office from stores at the district warehouse and he would like to accommodate her wishes. Eager to please his boss, Oscar readily agreed.

What happened after that was unbelievable, a personal "Pearl Harbor." First, Oscar got a history lesson. Soon after Mary came, Oscar learned from a number of sources that she was very well connected. Her brother was Allen Bitterman, builder and long-time school board member. Mary's sister was the vice president of the state teachers' organization. And Mary's steady "friend" was the attorney for the school district.

Oscar also learned that, early in her career, Mary had moved from one building to another. Several principals shared with Oscar that she had worked briefly for them and they were very relieved when she moved on. One even remarked that she was surprised that Mary lasted so long in her last position. With a wry smile, Amed Jones quipped, "I can't imagine how Jerry at stores put up with her for seven years."

This information was coupled with Oscar's assessment of Mary's performance. Her people skills were horrible. Her secretarial skills were nonexistent. Mary was rude and thoughtless. She often made mistakes—some serious. She was sloppy and undependable. She often came to work late and left early. Oscar first tried coaching; next, frank discussions with directives; and finally, reprimands. None of these strategies worked. Mary always mumbled compliance, and then went right back to doing the same unwanted behaviors. When Oscar turned to written directives with employee sign-off, timelines went unmet and papers mysteriously disappeared. Even Oscar's offer to help Mary relocate and find a more successful job placement was summarily rejected. Mary not only did not care, she felt secure and protected.

Oscar's efforts created an enemy. For every suggestion, direction, or chastisement Oscar meted out, Mary countered with inefficiency, backstabbing, and sabotage. When Oscar complained to his boss, Larry told him she was his problem and he should handle the matter. No one wanted to tangle with Mary. No one was there to help.

Well, this little phone call was the last incident. Oscar would not put up with this any longer. There was no tenure for secretaries. Who did she think she was? Oscar decided to approach the superintendent when he returned from the state capitol. Oscar would demand that he transfer or, better yet, fire Mary Bitterman. Superintendent Larry Hatcher would have to decide. Goodbye, Mary, or goodbye, Oscar.

Epilogue: Oscar did demand that the superintendent fire or transfer Mary. His boss explained that there were no available openings for transfer at the time and if Oscar wanted her fired he would have to do it himself. He explained that there was no secretaries' union and the board policy made Oscar her immediate supervisor, giving him the right to fire her. However, although the district would be glad to see her gone, Oscar was on his own with this.

Oscar understood that independently firing Mary was political suicide. He took no action.

Today, two bosses later, Mary still works for the district. Within a year of this event, Oscar took a position as an assistant superintendent in a different state.

HOW TAXING ARE SUCH ENCOUNTERS?

Those surveyed agreed that inevitably all people in positions of authority would encounter individuals who were their personal detractors. They felt these types of people were an aggravation and a frustration. They rated encounters with these backstabbers as a **3–stressful.**

However, when dealing with backstabbers who were immediate subordinates or close colleagues, this raised the stress level. Administrators participating in the study responded that when forced to work closely with a backstabber, stress mounts. Since the middle of the 20th century, the American educational system has accepted and practiced Fayol's Principles for Organizations (Gulick & Urwick, 1937; Kaiser, 2003; Kosmoski, 2001). We expect esprit de corps. We expect our subordinates to accept our authority, act as a team, follow the rules, and demonstrate loyalty to us and the organization. When this does not occur and these basic tenets are rejected, school administrators feel distraught. Survey participants emphasized that not being able to trust an individual with whom they had daily contact kept them off balance, agitated, and defensive. They rated this situation a **4–more stressful.**

5–most stressful	4–more stressful	3– stressful	2–little stress	1–no stress

A PSYCHOLOGICAL PERSPECTIVE OF THIS SITUATION: WHAT DO WE KNOW ABOUT MARY THE BACKSTABBER?

This Disabling the Backstabber vignette is a contemporary version of the Typhoid Mary story. Typhoid Mary was a carrier of typhoid fever who caused illness for many people. She refused to cooperate with authorities and would not allow herself to be isolated from others. As a result, hundreds suffered because they came in contact with her. Unlike Typhoid Mary, Mary the Backstabber never physically killed anyone, but she may have caused many their professional death.

We also know that no matter how good you are, no matter how professional you are, no matter how unfair it is, there are people who do have the ability to sabotage your career. How can they do this? Simply because they are better politically connected than you are.

Mary is much better connected than Oscar. Recall the axiom, Blood is thicker than water. Mary counts on her political connections to maintain her position. She knows her connections virtually assure her of a job as long as she wants it, or at least for as long as her brother remains on the school board. She also feels that her acts of sabotage will be ignored and left unpunished because of her powerful ties. This makes Mary very bold.

Even if Mary were certain she could not be removed from her position, this does not fully explain her behavior. Her behavior is best described as passive-aggressive. Such people can be the bane of our existence.

A number of Mary's actions typify passive-aggressive behavior. Mary's "forgetfulness" has the purpose of sabotaging Oscar's efforts. Mary further destroys Oscar's credibility by intentional inefficiency. One can count on her to be habitually late. She is late for work and late when completing given assignments. She habitually asks to leave work early. Her motto seems to be, "Arrive late, leave early." Finally, if Mary were directly confronted, she would stubbornly deny any knowledge of the difficulties between her and Oscar.

Although not considered a diagnostic category, the American Psychiatric Association (1994) describes individuals with Passive-Aggressive Personality Disorder or Negativistic Personality Disorder:

These individuals habitually resent, oppose, and resist demands to function at a level expected by others. This opposition occurs most frequently in work situations but can also be evident in social functioning. The resistance is expressed by procrastination, forgetfulness, stubbornness, and intentional inefficiency, especially in response to tasks assigned by authority figures. These individuals obstruct the efforts of others by failing to do their share of the work . . . . These individuals feel cheated, unappreciated, and misunderstood and ironically complain to others. When difficulties appear, they blame their failure on the behavior of others. They may be sullen, irritable, impatient, argumentative, cynical, skeptical, and contrary. Authority figures . . . often become the focus of discontent. (p. 733)

Although we can identify these passive-aggressive behaviors, we can only speculate on the reasons for Mary's actions. It could be because she wished that someone else had received Oscar's position. Or, perhaps, she does not feel she gets the respect from Oscar that she deserves. A third possibility is that she believes she knows more than Oscar knows, and, if only given the opportunity, that she could do a better job.

Because of her connections, Mary feels secure in her position and bold in her sabotage efforts. These actions are examples of passive-aggressive behavior. We can only speculate as to why Mary engages in these behaviors. We do know that she is very dangerous and can be lethal to an individual's career.

HOW WELL DID THE ADMINISTRATOR HANDLE THE BACKSTABBING SECRETARY?

A Practitioner's View

Poor Oscar Franks! How unfair! All of us can sympathize with Oscar's misfortune. Our initial reaction is that Oscar was ruined by outside forces that overwhelmed him—forces over which he had no control. Yet, on closer examination of the situation, we have to admit that Oscar himself was, to some degree, responsible for the retold events.

Oscar's first, and perhaps most lethal, mistake was agreeing to accept Mary as his secretary. Savvy administrators know how important it is to have a competent and loyal secretary or administrative assistant. They recognize that this key individual can be their greatest asset or their greatest liability.

A secretary can either protect, support, and defend you or attack, persecute, and fight you. He or she can be your champion or your foe. Given an opportunity to choose a secretary, Oscar should have insisted on choosing his own (Kosmoski, 1999b).

This leads to Oscar's second mistake. Oscar appears to be laboring under the misconception that he needs to honor all his boss's requests. He seems to think it proper to give his superordinate,

Superintendent Hatcher, anything he wants. In reality, a good subordinate should decline to acquiesce if the request from the boss could be damaging. Mary was obviously damaging to Oscar, Oscar's productivity, and the school district.

Next, Oscar Franks behaved poorly in the last conversation with Superintendent Hatcher. He should not have backed down and retreated. Rather, he should have explained how the situation was intolerable, unproductive, and damaging to all. Oscar should have insisted upon support from his boss. The vignette mentions that Oscar had a good six-year working relationship with Larry Hatcher. This implies the superintendent valued Oscar's ability and contributions. Oscar should, therefore, not underestimate his personal worth. This conversation was the time to demand respect and support from his boss.

Although we know it is wise to be flexible, there are times when we need to remain steadfast and unswerving. By meekly accepting his boss's refusal of help, Oscar further isolated himself from the team. Team approaches to resolving conflict in school settings are most productive (Burrello, Hoffman, & Murray, 2004). Oscar needed to stand his ground at this crucial juncture. Boldness, not timidity, was required.

Finally, after Oscar accepted the responsibility of firing Mary, he should have moved in that direction. Yes, firing someone is distasteful and stressful. Yes, it is dangerous, but sometimes we need to take risks. Probably the worst scenario to develop after firing Mary was that she would be gone and he would be asked to look elsewhere. So what! He couldn't perform well in this district as things stood, and others would be spared Mary's incompetence and backstabbing assaults. It is also possible such action could lead to a different conclusion. Oscar could weather and survive the inevitable backlash following his firing of Mary. If this happened, the entire district would be better off in the long run.

A Clinical View

The clinical view of how Oscar handled this backstabber differs from the practitioner's view on one major point. If Oscar had secured and utilized the services of a qualified mentor or peer confidant, he would never have accepted Mary as his secretary and she would not have been able to cause him such damage. This true story would have been avoided.

The current educational administration research clearly demonstrates that the acquisition and use of a mentor has great professional, psychological, and physiological benefits. The literature defines a qualified mentor as an individual who is highly successful in the field and has much experience to draw upon. Furthermore, the literature characterizes the mentor as a person willing to freely share his or her expertise with the mentee, or protégé (Kosmoski, 1999b; Kosmoski & Pollack, 1997, 1998).

In this case, a mentor would have been useful to Oscar. If Oscar had called upon his mentor before making the decision to accept Mary, it would have helped him avoid this major blunder. The initial discussion might have been as follows:

Oscar states, "I have been asked to hire a secretary named Mary at the request of Larry Hatcher."

Mentor replies, "Why?"

Oscar responds, "Because she wants to work in the central office." Oscar's mentor again asks, "Why?"

When Oscar cannot answer this question, his mentor has already given him the answer as to whether he should hire Mary or not. Given the choice of accepting a secretary of unknown loyalty and competency versus incurring the boss's displeasure or anger, the mentor would have undoubtedly recommended the latter. The mentor has been through many such dilemmas during the course of her or his career.

The value of finding and frequently utilizing a qualified mentor has been clearly documented in the literature (Collins, 2001; Covey, 1990; Kosmoski, 1999b). Mentees can call upon their mentors to discuss potentially debilitating choices before decisions are made. If you have not done so already, you should seriously resolve to find and utilize a qualified mentor. Remember, a school system is a living, breathing, political animal that can be as loyal as an Irish wolfhound or as dangerous as a rattlesnake.

ADDITIONAL SUGGESTIONS: WHAT ELSE COULD AND SHOULD YOU DO IN SIMILAR SITUATIONS?

1. Preparation before this kind of confrontation is essential. We are unclear about Oscar's support system. We know that in

crucial situations such as this one, a wide and reliable support base is critical. Correctly anticipating constituent attitudes and behaviors is invaluable (Pryor & Pryor, 2004). Prudent administrators need to spend time developing personal and professional relationships, to be called upon when necessary. Respect and support from school board members, colleagues, staff, and the community at large allow the administrator the option of taking decisive action. In this vignette, Oscar's only support resource appears to be his superintendent, Larry Hatcher. Over his six-year tenure in the district, Oscar should have broadened his support network and then drawn upon it during this time of need.

2. Prior to challenging Mary's actions and position, Oscar needed to build his case. Again, documentation is necessary. He should have noted and sorted conclusive evidence from unsupported notions (Bruer, 1998).

3. In situations when firing is a genuine and, perhaps, desirable outcome, it is wise to use the existing bureaucracy. Hiring and firing is the prerogative of the school board. In this case, Oscar should have presented his case to them for joint action. Administrators faced with individuals who should be removed from their positions must rely on the procedures and mechanisms in place.

4. In the epilogue, we learned that Oscar moved on by choice, while Mary remained. Obviously, Oscar had made a conscious decision to remove himself from what he considered an unbearable situation. However, he did not fulfill his responsibility for the good of the district. Oscar has a moral obligation to free the district of Mary, a major damaging force. This is not vindictive behavior but, rather, it is ethical behavior on the part of an individual in authority. By firing Mary before he departed, Oscar Franks would have saved many others pain and humiliation. He would have improved working conditions, effectiveness, and, ultimately, the success of the school district.

IN WHAT OTHER CASES DO THE LEARNED TECHNIQUES APPLY?

Backstabbers come from a multitude of positions. They may be found in the ranks of bosses, peers, teachers, and parents. Some may be strategically placed, as Mary was, while others can be mere acquaintances. For those far removed from our everyday chores, our colleagues suggest several strategies.

If you become aware of an isolated attack, ignore it. Don't waste your time or energy. However, if an individual is frequently misinterpreting or undermining your position or reputation, action is warranted. Candidly and privately face the backstabber. Explain what information you have and inform the person that you find erroneous, unsupported, and venomous comments unacceptable. Tell the person you would prefer not to have to oppose him or her publicly if further incidents occur. Assure the individual that future unfounded or unfair remarks will result in consequences. Express your wish to forget past occurrences and start afresh. Often, this direct confrontation will defuse the backstabber.

If an individual persists after you have spoken directly to him or her, try this approach. Avoid as much direct contact as possible. It is more difficult for a backstabber to malign you if they have no direct information. If you must meet with the individual, try to do so in front of witnesses. Respond to hearsay with the truth. Use a calm and detached demeanor. Finally, learn to live with it. Don't let one bitter individual control you or your effectiveness.

SUMMARY

- In general, we find encounters with backstabbers taxing. The closer we have to work with the disloyal individual, the higher the level of stress.
- Do not underestimate the gravity of the situation if a backstabber is a close coworker, such as your secretary. A venomous individual can cause your professional demise.
- Remember, there are pathological people who are not going to respond to your ministrations. They do not have the ability or desire to do so. Sometimes the only solution is termination.
- One of the best ways to avoid making costly mistakes is heeding the advice of a qualified mentor. Seriously seek your own mentor.

SUGGESTED READINGS

Finding and Utilizing a Qualified Mentor

Collins, J. (2001). *Good to great: Why some companies make the leap . . . and others don't.* New York: Harper Collins.

Covey, S. R. (1990). *Seven habits of highly effective people: Powerful lessons in personal change.* New York: Franklin Covey.

Kosmoski, G. J. (1999). *How to land the best jobs in school administration* (Rev. ed.). Thousand Oaks, CA: Corwin.

Learning to Predict Attitudes of Constituents

Kosmoski, G. J., & Pollack, D. R. (Speakers). (1998, February/March). *From Jekyll to Hyde: The changes of beginning school administrators* (Cassette Recording No. AASA98–80). American Association of School Administrators 130th National Conference on Education, San Diego, CA.

Pryor, P. W., & Pryor, C. R. (2004). *The school leaders' guide to understanding attitude and influencing behavior: Working with teachers, parents, students, and the community.* Thousand Oaks, CA: Corwin Press.

Meeting the Challenge of Volatile Educational Issues

THE STORY: Dealing With the Challenge of No Child Left Behind

THE PLACE: A Northwest City Faced With Recent High-Tech Layoffs

Pearl Sandels was curious and slightly apprehensive as she welcomed Jonathan Grimmer into her office. She had no idea what had prompted him to visit her this afternoon. Yesterday, all he had said to her secretary was that he wanted a private meeting with her as soon as possible. He refused to indicate the topic he wished to discuss.

Jonathan Grimmer was one of the three new school board members elected last month. At his first general board meeting, he had not mentioned any concerns or issues that he wanted to discuss with her as superintendent. Each time they had met during the campaign and after the election, Jonathan Grimmer was polite, cordial, and, yes, friendly. Pearl's initial reaction to him was positive.

Late yesterday afternoon, Pearl called Ira Cohen, who had served as a board member for three terms. He had the most seniority on the present board. Ira was a fair, bright, and well-respected man who had his finger on the pulse of the entire district. Pearl had a good working relationship with Ira during the six years she had been superintendent. She felt comfortable asking Ira if he had any knowledge about Grimmer's request for a private meeting. Unfortunately, Ira couldn't provide her with any insight. So here she was, about to take part in a meeting with no preparation or background knowledge. Pearl didn't like surprises when it came to her job. Still, she willed herself not to fall into the trap of speculation without facts. She would keep an open mind.

Now, Grimmer faced her while sitting in the armchair across the coffee table from her. They had spent a few minutes making small talk and complimenting each other. They were now calling each other by their first names.

After another sip of his tea, Jonathan gave her a wry smile and said, "I know you're busy, so let me get to the point of this meeting. Last weekend, Maria Sanchez, Gus Vassar, and I got together at my beach house to discuss district issues and came to some decisions."

"You know we ran and won as a coalition. Our message was simple. This district will meet 'No Child Left Behind' goals. We are now the voice of NCLB for this district. We felt it was only fair to tell you what that is going to mean over the next four years. Our group appointed me to inform you and, later today, our current board president of our decision."

Now serious in voice and demeanor, Grimmer continued, "Our test scores are no longer the best in the area. Sure, they're pretty good, but not the best. We want to be the best and won't settle for anything else. All we see is that the test scores have started to drop."

Pearl leaned forward and broke in, "Wait a moment. Our test scores aren't just 'pretty good.' They are very good. You know we have lost a significant number of long-term high-performing students because of business closings and family relocations over the last two years. And I'm sure the three of you know that we have gained a significant number of disadvantaged students because of the shifting population. Those being the facts, we should be very proud of our performance on all measures, including the required state test."

"That's all smoke and mirrors! You and I both know that the kids could do much better and have the best scores in the state if only you, your principals, and your teachers would get off your duffs, try harder, and do what we pay you to do. If people want to keep their jobs, they better show us results. Stop the bleeding! Otherwise, be prepared to go job hunting!" retorted Jonathan Grimmer.

Before she could respond, Grimmer growled, "If you don't think we can do it, you're wrong. There might only be three of us united in this action now, but we can be very vocal and won't hesitate to go public. That gives us unbelievable power and will surely move one or two of our 'peace-loving' board members over to our way of thinking."

Pearl was furious but replied calmly, "Let me make sure I have this right. First, you claim that because you ran on an NCLB platform, the district test scores are no longer good enough and that they must improve significantly before you will be satisfied."

Grimmer nodded and she continued, "Second, you blame the small drop in scores not on changing demographics but on the lack of effort and effectiveness of my administrators and teachers."

"Correct!" spat out Grimmer. "And don't forget that we can lay the lion's share of fault at your feet."

Despite his outbursts, Pearl persisted, "Well Mr. Grimmer, I believe you have made yourself perfectly clear. And obviously we do not agree on this issue at all. At this time, we appear to be poles apart. I think we need some time to cool down and think through our positions. Perhaps we can schedule a meeting with the entire board next week and come to some understanding."

Jonathan Grimmer jumped to his feet. Coldly he replied, "This was a private 'heads up.' I have no desire to share this information publicly at this time. This discussion was strictly between you and me. To everyone else, this meeting never happened. You would be wise not to try to force my hand in this matter. You'd be better off using your time to get the test scores up where they belong. We want the best. Got it? Good day, Superintendent Sandels."

With that said, Mr. Grimmer stepped across the room, opened the office door, and closed it gently behind himself.

Epilogue: Fighting anger and anxiety, Pearl took two days to calm down and assess the situation. She realized her need to be proactive and decisive and formulated a plan of action. Here follows her actions over the next month.

1. After formulating her tentative course of action, Pearl met with her husband of 22 years, Paul, and she shared her thoughts and potential actions with him. She knew that whatever plan she adopted, there could be life-changing effects for her whole family. Pearl was relieved and bolstered by her husband when he whole-heartedly agreed to support her plan and subsequent course of action.

2. Pearl met with the district board president. She was glad that they had come to respect and trust each other over the years. She related in detail the content of her meeting with Jonathan Grimmer. She also explained the facts of the district performance related to No Child Left Behind (NCLB) issues. Pearl frankly expressed her disgust with Grimmer himself. She cited his ignorance, unfair "axe grinding," and unethical threats against her employees, members of the board, and herself. She made it clear that she would neither be party to nor be intimidated by any such backroom political antics. She insisted that this issue, faulty logic, and false accusations should be addressed directly and forcefully. Pearl persuaded the board president to call an executive board meeting where she would report to all board members on the state of the district as it complied with and met NCLB and state goals and standards.

3. At the executive meeting, Pearl made it a point to give information, explain changing conditions, and review the competent and achievable plan for progress designed by representative district constituents. Giving concrete examples, she emphasized the effort and effectiveness of the district personnel. Last, Pearl Sandels strongly urged the board to actively spread the good news of their successes to the entire community.

4. Finally, Pearl and the board president hosted a press-covered town forum where they shared the district's "NCLB Good News Report." The press reported positively. Even Jonathan Grimmer and his cronies went on record as praising Pearl and her entire educational team.

5. Pearl and her husband celebrated a job well done with a quiet dinner at home. For the first time in a good month, Pearl got to sleep before 2:00 a.m. and slept through the night without nightmares.

HOW TAXING ARE SUCH ENCOUNTERS?

This scenario touches upon two issues that qualify as hostile conversations. First is the forever-present confrontation with unscrupulous and/or irrational superordinates or power elite. Power elite is defined as those individuals in a community with considerable influence, power, and control over political, social, and economic decisions (Estep, 2003). Astute administrative leaders should not believe the myth that an individual who has many responsibilities and a commanding position is necessarily fair, just, rational, and, most important, ethical. Rather, they have the right and duty to confront questionable behavior. Colleagues view this type of hostile encounter as extremely threatening and, therefore, categorize it as a **5–most stressful.**

The second issue posed in this story is the emerging trend in education of tying employment to student performance. In a survey we conducted during the summer of 2003, 250 practicing and aspiring administrators reported an encounter of this type as being the *most* dreaded and feared. By a margin of two to one, practitioners and "wannabes" alike rate this situation as the most stressful, again earning this scenario a 5 on the stress scale.

5–most stressful	4–more stressful	3– stressful	2–little stress	1–no stress

A PSYCHOLOGICAL PERSPECTIVE OF THIS SITUATION: WHAT DO WE KNOW ABOUT NO CHILD LEFT BEHIND?

The NCLB Act has placed a very weighty burden on all educators (Ambrosio, 2004). The demands placed upon Dr. Sandels by the nature of her job alone are difficult to manage. The demands placed upon her by the NCLB Act have added to that burden. For example, some of the effects of the NCLB Act upon her school district are to (a) ensure that her students perform to a standard that is not necessarily designed for the needs of her district, (b) require increased performance without any increase in funding, and (c) operate under the threat of a reduction in funding if some children fail. This last effect has a profound impact. Much of her ability to set priorities and controls over her district has been removed from her, her teachers, and her staff. The focus of her school district has changed from the broad concept of educating students to "teaching to the test." No matter how hard she may work to improve her district scores on standardized tests, her district may be defined as failing by someone outside of her district.

Although the literature suggests numerous positive outcomes from NCLB, no matter how well intentioned the legislation, it is likely to have many unintended negative consequences because of reduced local control. Karasek (1979) found that when job demands are rated high but employee control is rated low, employees report exhaustion after work, trouble awakening in the morning, depression, nervousness, anxiety, and insomnia or disturbed sleep. Rather than enhancing personal control over the workplace, NCLB has reduced control over the workplace. Hackman and Oldham (1976) found that 94% of workers consider autonomy and independence to be more important than job satisfaction. In 2003, Wasserstein, Shea, Mulhern, and Field found independence/autonomy to be a condition of job satisfaction for faculties. Based on these findings, we can expect the NCLB Act to drive highly qualified educators out of public schools because of the lack of control. Dr. Sandels is well aware of the profound changes NCLB will have on her district and her staff. She knows that parents are apprehensive about the consequences on their children. Rather than supporting Dr. Sandels, the district, the parents, and the children, the Grimmer group has added to the burden. This is a time of profound educational change and unrest. Unlike Mr. Grimmer, we all need to be involved with and supportive of one another. We don't want to lose the positives we presently have, whether they be administrators, teachers, or students, while adjusting to the new reality of education.

It is important to note that psychologists, as well as other professionals, believe that their role in education will increase due to NCLB. Psychologists are particularly interested in the provision that allows them to intervene if a school fails to progress two years in a row. In this scenario, the school district will act as broker, matching low-achieving students with outside professionals. The NCLB Act allows academic services to be provided by a professional such as a private practice psychologist (Kersting, 2004), thereby taking the control of education from educators.

HOW WELL DID THE ADMINISTRATOR HANDLE THIS THREAT?

A Practitioner's View

In this confrontation, Pearl Sandels superbly demonstrates why she is a long-term superintendent. Her overall behavior is that of a seasoned, knowledgeable, and confident administrator. Some of her actions that support this conclusion are her efforts to gather information before the meeting with Mr. Grimmer, her ability to remain calm even when frustrated and furious, and her use of paraphrasing during the discussion in order to clarify the issues.

Pearl also showed remarkable restraint when choosing her actions after the meeting. She did not rush ahead thoughtlessly. Rather, she took the time to determine her actions. Then she chose a process (a number of related activities designed to reach a goal) that she reasoned would be successful. Pearl needs to be commended for discussing her plan with her husband before acting. Sensitive to the gravity of the situation, she recognized that this conflict could have major consequences for her family and, therefore, included her husband in her decision. Finally, Pearl, like other successful leaders, appears to have established her credibility and expertise long before the actual incident. This scenario makes it clear that she had spent many hours over many years building trust and a positive working relationship with the veteran board members. That she could speak candidly with the board president and have him support her plan shows that she had earned his respect and trust.

There is one word of caution. Pearl Sandels may have won this battle, but the issues and controversy surrounding NCLB are just beginning. Also, misguided and misinformed zealots will always be around to challenge sincere and competent administrators. In this scenario, it seems clear that Jonathan Grimmer is not the type of man to forgive and forget. Rather, he probably views this as a setback rather than a defeat. Experts have proven that people with power are more likely to revisit and escalate existing conflicts than people with less power (Glomb, 2002). Pearl can be quite sure that this issue and his unethical and onerous threat will rise again before his term of office expires.

The only criticism one can make of Superintendent Sandels's behavior is noted in the last sentence of the epilogue: "For the first time in a good month, Pearl got to sleep before 2:00 a.m. and slept through the night without nightmares." This statement suggests that she could not put the encounter and subsequent actions out of her mind and "give it a rest." A dedicated and competent administrator must learn to deal with situations during working hours and then let them go when it's time to rest. Sleeplessness and disturbing dreams only sap one's strength. These actions are damaging to the individual's physical and emotional health. Richard M. Suinn (2001), in his article "The Terrible Twos: Anger and Anxiety Hazardous to Your Health," unequivocally demonstrates that anger and anxiety affect health and mortality. Furthermore, he shows that there are effective interventions to combat the states of anger and anxiety. It would be useful for Pearl to learn and systematically practice anxiety-reduction exercises, relaxation techniques, and stress-relieving activities. The Grimmers in our lives are not worth risking hypertension, high blood pressure, or worse.

A Clinical View

Mr. Grimmer's NCLB triumvirate was elected to the school board in an attempt to influence the direction of the school district with regard to a specific issue. As board members, the three united gained power and strength. As a team, he and his allies were planning to bully Dr. Sandels into submission to their wishes. Emotionally abusive behavior, such as Mr. Grimmer's threats, negatively affects the victim's sense of self as a competent person and causes a sense of humiliation. Benedict Carey's (2004) interviews of Drs. Garey Namie, Harvey A. Hornstein, and Michelle Duffy conclude that adult bullies who are in positions of power are just as likely to pick on a strong subordinate as a weak one. Most often, people in positions of authority bully for the sheer pleasure of exercising power. Unfortunately, those who work for bullies frequently become less sensitive over time. They begin to feel more alone and isolated, making them easier to manipulate in the future.

Dr. Sandels immediately responds proactively to the initial threat rather than taking an inappropriately defensive position and thereby falling into Mr. Grimmer's trap. The American Psychological Association (2004), in its Psychology Matters website, states that Stanley Milgram's work suggests four specific actions for resisting unwanted pressures from authorities: (a) question the authority's legitimacy; (b) when asked to do something that you consider wrong, ask yourself if the activity requested of you is something that you would do on your own; (c) do not start to comply with activities with which you feel uncomfortable; and (d) if you find the behavior repugnant or objectionable, find yourself an ally who shares your perceptions and is willing to join you in opposing that behavior.

The secrecy demand that Mr. Grimmer places upon Dr. Sandels leaves her in a very vulnerable and uncomfortable position. If she remains passive and maintains the secrecy of her meeting with Mr. Grimmer, she endangers her relationship with the board chairman and the board as a whole. Neither would want to hear secondhand about a secret meeting that she had with an individual whose agenda varies with that of the board as a whole. Pearl takes a positive action. She informs her board president of the situation and threat to her and, by implication, to the board president. Together, they cement their relationship with the community by having a public meeting in which they discuss the issues raised by Mr. Grimmer. They share their good news with the community as well as the difficulties faced under NCLB. By her actions, Dr. Sandels demonstrates her expertise and professionalism. If she is available, you should hire her.

ADDITIONAL SUGGESTIONS: WHAT ELSE COULD AND SHOULD YOU DO IN SIMILAR SITUATIONS?

We must become experts on the NCLB tenets, ramifications, and legislative requirement. NCLB requirements will be a priority in schools across the country. It is impossible for today's educators to deny the fact that we face the difficult and challenging dilemma of meeting higher expectations and standards while getting diminished resources. Meeting the demand for measurable and tangible results required by NCLB regulations is among the most urgent issues confronting virtually every U.S. school system (Association of Supervision and Curriculum Development, 2004). School leaders must be knowledgeable about issues and initiatives that will shape many of our local practices. In this scenario, two issues touched upon are closing the achievement gap between disadvantaged students and their wealthier peers and equating test scores to improved performance. As administrators, we need to learn about topics such as "When Do Children Fall Behind?" and "What Can Be Done?" (Davison, Young, Davenport, Butterbaugh, & Davison, 2004) as well as "How Does Measurement Improve School Performance?" (Anderson, MacDonald, & Sinnemann, 2004).

In this real scenario, Pearl Sandels's actions worked and there was a positive outcome—a happy ending. However, this is not necessarily the case in all such situations. A serious administrator must be realistic when it comes to job retention. Statistics supplied by the American Association of School Administrators show that the national average tenure for school superintendents is 6.8 years, with urban district superintendents serving, on average, only 2.5 years (Oglesby, 2001). Principals, too, have little permanency. In 2000, public school principals had an average of 9 years in the position but served, on average, in 2.7 buildings during that time span (Gates, Ringel, Santibanez, Chung, & Ross, 2003). Women and minorities, on average, have less tenure in a given position than their male counterparts.

Even when administrators are right or act appropriately, their jobs are not necessarily protected or secure. Good administrators are fired for reasons beyond their control and not always based upon their performance of duties. Other factors, such as change in goals and directions, new superordinates, or reduction in the workforce, affect administrators' employment. It is suggested that today's administrator recognize this possibility and accept the risk before committing to this challenging career.

IN WHAT OTHER CASES DO THE LEARNED TECHNIQUES APPLY?

This scenario explores two general problems: (a) dealing with an unscrupulous yet very powerful advisory and (b) confronting emerging and potentially volatile school issues. When engaged in disagreement with any powerful combatant, school administrators may successfully use a number of techniques employed by Superintendent Sandels. These include clarifying the issues by making sure you have the facts, remaining in control of yourself, developing a logical plan and process to deal with the situation, and gathering the support and efforts of other team members. Many individuals have great influence over school affairs. Besides board members, they include the media; politicians; leaders in business; and representatives of civic, community, and parent groups. Clearly, one wishes to have the support of such individuals. However, if these people oppose you or your position, it is wise to move cautiously and thoughtfully.

As educators, the one thing we can be sure of is change. And with change often comes confusion, controversy, and apprehension. NCLB is truly an issue of change directly affecting schools today. However, it is not the only challenge and it will certainly not be the last. Today's administrator must be aware and knowledgeable of national trends, initiatives, and new discoveries. Only by being cognizant will school administrators make good futuristic local decisions. A few examples of potentially volatile issues at both the national and local level are school choice, alternative teacher certification, and national competency testing. Regardless of the current issue, knowledge and the ability to relate it to your given situation is key.

SUMMARY

- Lay the groundwork before conflict. Regardless of the location or success of any district, eventually administrators will be confronted with unscrupulous, opinionated, and/or irrational powerful adversaries. Do not underestimate the damage such individuals can cause to you or your organization. Building a support base and a positive reputation before such incidents is essential.
- Change is an integral part of education. Therefore, we should expect and embrace the challenge of controversial and potentially volatile educational issues.
- The magnitude of NCLB and the potential threat of tying employment to student test performance is a real nationwide

concern of current practitioners. Examine the facts and determine your own position on this issue.

- Good communication skills, reflection, and decisiveness are invaluable tools when engaged in disagreements with a powerful advisory. Understanding and accepting the fact that there is little permanency in administrative positions is "freeing," and a proactive approach to personal employment.

- A highly charged conflict, like the one in this scenario, is both emotionally and physically taxing. School administrators must develop strategies and practices to curb the terrible two—anger and anxiety—to improve their quality of life (Kosmoski, Pollack, & Schmidt, 1999).

- Awareness of the current state of affairs, proven practices, and new initiatives make school administrators leaders with vision (Cambron-McCabe, Cunningham, Harvey, & Koff, 2004; Hoyle, Bjork, Collier, & Glass, 2004).

SUGGESTED READINGS

Understanding the Gravity and Personal, Physical, and Emotional Effects of Highly Charged Confrontations

Kosmoski, G. J., Pollack, D. R., & Schmidt, L. J. (1999). Jekyll or Hyde: Changes in leadership styles and the personalities of beginning school administrators. *Illinois Schools Journal, 79*(1), 23–34.

Suinn, R. M. (2001). The terrible twos: Anger and anxiety hazardous to your health. *American Psychology, 56*(1), 27–36.

Understanding the Challenge of a Career in School Administration

Gates, S. M., Ringel, J. S., Santibanez, L., Chung, C. H., & Ross, K. (2003). *Who is leading our schools? An overview of school administrators and their careers.* New York: Rand.

Hoyle, J. R., Bjork, L. G., Collier, V., & Glass, T. (2004). *The superintendent as CEO: Standard-based performance.* Thousand Oaks, CA: Corwin with AASA.

Understanding the Challenges of NCLB

Ambrosio, J. (2004). No Child Left Behind: The case of Roosevelt High School. *Phi Delta Kappan, 85*(9), 709–712.

Cambron-McCabe, N., Cunningham, L. L., Harvey, J., & Koff, R. H. (2004). *The superintendents' fieldbook: A guide for leaders of learning.* Thousand Oaks, CA: Corwin with AASA.

CHAPTER ELEVEN

Maintaining Confidentiality

THE STORY: Forced Silence

THE PLACE: The North Central School District Board Room

Dr. William Gladhand waved goodbye to his various administrators as they gathered their paraphernalia and departed
for their respective buildings. Bill Gladhand was pleased with the
results of his "A-team" (administrative) meeting. He had conducted
an extensive amount of business in the past three hours and was
satisfied with the team's progress. Even Terry Burns, principals'
representative and one of his senior building administrators, had
very few questions or grievances this morning.

Bill was trying to decide what he would do for lunch when
Terry Burns tapped him on the shoulder. Looking around, Bill saw
that the room had emptied and the two of them were now alone.

"Dr. Gladhand, there's one more issue I'd like to discuss," Terry
began. "A number of our administrators have come to me about a
rumor that has been circulating throughout the district in the past
couple of days. It seems they have heard that you will be proposing
a districtwide dress code for the fall. Any truth to that?" Terry
asked.

Dr. William Gladhand shook his head and smiled. Putting his hand on Terry's shoulder, he steered him toward the door. In a friendly, conversational tone, he replied, "What are you talking about? Terry, you know full well that I would never consider instituting any sweeping change without first consulting my A-team. We don't have any secrets here."

Bill was now parallel with his own office door. He turned the door handle, slipped inside, and escaped from Terry. Bill sighed deeply. Being superintendent of schools was not always easy. He found it difficult to be anything less than direct and forthright—especially with people he admired and had come to trust. Still, he had given his word to keep silent.

Three weeks later, Terry Burns flipped to the local news section in his morning paper. His attention became riveted to the following headline: "Call for Public Hearings! School Board Instructs Superintendent to Explore Dress Code by Fall."

HOW TAXING ARE SUCH ENCOUNTERS?

This vignette addresses the issue of confidentiality. When speaking to Terry Burns, Dr. William Gladhand knew the school board would institute a new dress code policy. The board had instructed Bill to remain silent until they could make the public announcement. Bill could not share the news with anyone—including his A-team.

As school administrators, we are often privy to confidential information. Some could be potentially damaging, highly volatile, or politically delicate.

When directly challenged to reveal a confidence, the administrators polled felt that keeping information private was quite taxing. They specifically balked at situations requiring them to be less than direct, candid, and forthright. As a group, they gave maintaining confidentiality a surprisingly high stress rating of **4–more stressful.**

5–most stressful	4–more stressful	3–stressful	2–little stress	1–no stress

A PSYCHOLOGICAL PERSPECTIVE OF THIS SITUATION: WHAT DO WE KNOW ABOUT THE PRESSURES OF MAINTAINING CONFIDENTIALITY?

This is a very repugnant situation. There are split loyalties in this scenario. Dr. Gladhand has a responsibility to the school board and a responsibility to his A-team. As superintendent, Dr. Gladhand must first meet the demands of the board. If the board requires secrecy for specific issues, then he must meet those demands.

Dr. Gladhand's problems began with his A-team. The scenario paints a picture of a unique group of people constituting the A-team. By his words and actions, he has set up certain expectations for the A-team members. Terry Burns's expectation is that Dr. Gladhand will share all information and, accordingly, he seeks information from Dr. Gladhand concerning a rumor he has heard. Dr. Gladhand's response is to lie to him, thereby keeping the confidence of the board but destroying his credibility with his principals' representative and the A-team.

Dr. Gladhand's primary mistake was to raise expectations to a level that he could not meet. He implied by his statements and behavior that he was going to manage the school district in a collegial manner. However, when confronted with the situation of split loyalties, it became clear his administrative style was one of pseudo-collegiality. It is a style that on the surface is collegial and allows him to claim he is being contemporary in his administrative approach. In fact, he was not. It would have been better for Dr. Gladhand to discuss the purpose of the A-team at the beginning and the limitations placed upon him by his school board. The A-team would have understood and there would be no frustration on their part.

HOW WELL DID THE ADMINISTRATOR HANDLE CONFIDENTIALITY?

A Practitioner's View

Dr. William Gladhand did what many school administrators do in similar circumstances. Bill felt himself in an untenable position—a lose-lose situation. Regardless of which choice he made, there would be negative ramifications. He behaved as if there were only two choices; deceive Terry or deceive the board. Tell a "white lie" or break an unspoken oath. In his mind, he chose the lesser of two evils. By responding to Terry Burns in the way he did, Bill Gladhand bent the truth. He was not forthright. Although, technically, he did not directly lie to his subordinate, Dr. Gladhand's remarks were designed to misdirect or mislead. Apparently, he believed this was less egregious than betraying the confidence of the school board.

Dr. Gladhand was wrong. He made a critical mistake that led to an unsatisfactory conclusion. Dr. William Gladhand underestimated Terry Burns. He underestimated Terry both personally and professionally. The vignette made it clear that Terry Burns was a veteran building principal and a leader among his fellow principals. Terry, therefore, is neither stupid nor naive. Undoubtedly, Terry Burns has leadership qualities. Educational leaders are trustworthy, loyal, and savvy (Kosmoski & Pollack, 1999; Mackie, 1990; Ryan & Bohlin, 1999). Bill Gladhand should have taken these facts into account before responding to Terry's inquiry.

Admittedly, time to reflect and hindsight make this conversation much easier. Dr. Gladhand had neither luxury. Had he, he might have realized that there was a third and better solution. Consider this response. When Terry asked if there was any truth to the rumor, Dr. Gladhand might have said, "Terry, I'm not at liberty to discuss it at this time. When I can, I'll let you know. For now, I'd appreciate it if you could just keep the lid on." This, then, solves the ethical dilemma. Bill Gladhand would have told the truth and kept a confidence at the same time. There would be no further problem.

A second critical mistake Dr. Gladhand made was not repairing the damage caused by his little lie. As a human being, Dr. Gladhand, like all of us, makes mistakes, but he must learn to take responsibility for those mistakes and try to rectify them as much as possible. After the school board made its announcement, Bill should have spoken to Terry Burns. He did not. By not explaining and apologizing to Terry for his mistake, Bill Gladhand further damaged their relationship. In his position as superintendent, Bill Gladhand should be a role model for all his A-team members (Kaiser, 2003; Williams, 1985). He needs to model the behaviors he expects from his team. He did not, and then he did not take ownership for his behavior. When a superordinate acts in a dishonest and untrustworthy manner, he or she permanently scars relationships and the working climate (Levinas, 1995).

A Clinical View

Here is another way to approach this situation. You are stuck. You serve at the beneficence or the whim of the school board. While you have concern for the A-team, they have not hired you. This being said, you must deal with the issue of trust. You have no choice but to break trust. Dr. Gladhand has made an implied contract that he cannot keep. The result is that he decided to lie to Terry Burns. Now the issue is whether he has irrevocably lost basic trust or whether the A-team is willing to understand the dilemma in which Dr. Gladhand found himself.

Another way of looking at this situation is to compare the expectations of the unwritten contract between Dr. Gladhand and his A-team and the contract between a superstar baseball player and a team owner. The owner pays the athlete millions of dollars with the expectation that one in every three times at bat the player will get a hit. From the very beginning, the owner knows the player is not going to get a hit 100% of the time. Instead, he believes the player is going to get a hit 33% of the time. The owner has realistic expectations.

Dr. Gladhand has, unfortunately, set up the expectation with the A-team that he is going to share with them 100% of the information being discussed at school board meetings. This was unnecessary and unrealistic. Most of us do not have that expectation of a superintendent. We would be pleased if he shared 75% of the information available to him. The problem is that Dr. Gladhand, in his inimitable way, set up this expectation and, in doing so, jeopardized the bond of trust between himself and the A-team.

After the damage was done, Dr. Gladhand's best approach would have been to schedule a meeting with the A-team on the day of the announcement so that he could inform them of the school board's decision rather than have them find out from the newspaper or by word of mouth. At the meeting, he should have admitted that he raised levels of expectations beyond what he could reasonably uphold. He needs to explain that there will be future confidences that he cannot share. People are willing to forgive you when you cannot control the situation. Apologize and go on.

ADDITIONAL SUGGESTIONS: WHAT ELSE COULD AND SHOULD YOU DO IN SIMILAR SITUATIONS?

1. Basic trust is a fundamental need. We all need to be trusted. And, unless proven otherwise, we need to trust in the integrity and savvy of our close colleagues. When asked to share sensitive information by your associates, respond honestly that you are unable to comply. Good school administrators will understand and support your position. Your candor will strengthen professional and personal relationships.

2. Many frustrating situations may be completely avoided with solid preplanning and thorough procedures. If the superintendent, along with the school board, had developed a timeline and method for informing administrators prior to the announcement, the entire problem would have been moot.

3. If you find yourself challenged to divulge private information by an outsider, your position and responsibility changes. You must decide how much you should trust the outsider and the degree of sensitivity of the information. Then you can respond according to your assessment. Preparing in advance your responses to a variety of situations helps. Your mental collection of readily available responses should range from pleasant but noncommittal to candid. These comments would allow you to respond obliquely and truthfully without betraying the confidence. A few examples include, "I really don't know how to respond to that," "I'm not at liberty to discuss this," "Gee, I don't know," "What I know I was told in confidence and therefore I can't discuss it," and "It's an interesting rumor." Add to this short list. Self-reflection is one technique to utilize when building your collection. Spend a few minutes creating your own mental list. Yet another way to find helpful phrases is by asking friends and colleagues to share their favorite responses. You can then call up the response which best fits the situation and your own personality and style. Rehearse.

4. Avoid being wordy. Practicing administrators advise us to say as little as possible. When you are forced to respond to something you promised to keep confidential, don't pad or

ramble. Keep your response as brief and succinct as possible. Then, as quickly as possible, move the conversation to other topics. Often, individuals find themselves in difficulty because they talk too much. This is not the time to volunteer any information.

5. Explain and apologize when appropriate. This vignette ends with a confidence becoming public. On those occasions, when it is no longer necessary to remain silent, it is sometimes appropriate to share what transpired with the person who made the inquiry. In this case, Dr. Gladhand needed to apologize to Terry for misleading him. It would have been best for him to explain the facts to his entire A-team prior to the public airing in the newspapers. This type of behavior will work for you. Explanations and apologies will not change mistakes made when you handle a situation poorly, but they will often help repair damaged feelings and relationships (Williams, 1985).

6. Understand that you will be put in situations where confidentiality can never be breached. You will never be at liberty to share certain information. In these cases, you must accept the responsibility and behave as the professional you are.

7. Accept that you are human. If you are put in a similar uncomfortable situation and make mistakes, learn from the mistakes and move on. Do not punish yourself for being less than perfect. None of us enjoys admitting our failures, but they do happen. Do not compound the mistake by inordinate rumination and excessive self-chastisement. These behaviors are unproductive and injurious.

IN WHAT OTHER CASES DO
THE LEARNED TECHNIQUES APPLY?

School administrators often find themselves in situations requiring confidentiality. Less frequently, we are challenged or pressured to reveal the information we have agreed to keep private. Although infrequent, this situation does happen to all of us. Some situations that require our discretion are special education proceedings and decisions, legal actions, personnel issues, negotiations, and administrative/board strategies.

Most school administrators are approached by individuals (staff, parents, students, etc.) who wish to share information but with the understanding that it is to be held in confidence. Be cautious before you agree. Sometimes it is inappropriate or impossible to keep your word. Therefore, move slowly at the onset. Think before you engage in this type of agreement.

SUMMARY

- School administrators agree that the frustration and stress levels experienced when pressured to divulge confidential matters are high.
- Good administrators understand the necessity for confidentiality. They will neither be surprised nor disappointed if you refuse to share sensitive information. Be candid. Tell your savvy colleagues directly when you are bound to silence. They will applaud your integrity.
- Some practices that help school administrators handle this situation more professionally and painlessly are preparing response statements in advance, avoiding wordiness, and, when appropriate, explaining the situation after the fact.
- Administrators know there will be occasions when they are misunderstood and possibly maligned for not breaching confidentiality. Learn to live with it.
- School administrators must realize that they are human and, therefore, not perfect. They need to move on after making a mistake.

SUGGESTED READING

Mackie, J. L. (1990). *Ethics: Inventing right and wrong.* New York: Penguin.

CHAPTER TWELVE

What Works
in All Cases

THE 15 MOST OFTEN USED
STRATEGIES WHEN ENGAGED
IN DIFFICULT, FRUSTRATING,
OR HOSTILE CONVERSATIONS

After reviewing the previous chapters, it becomes apparent that
there are some practices or strategies helpful in most difficult situations. Having a mental list of those techniques would be most
helpful to all administrators. We would be much more efficient at
defusing unwanted and unnecessary hostile conversations if we
could learn what actually works. But what strategies do practicing
school administrators find most valuable?

To determine which strategies successful and effective leaders
utilize most often during hostile conversations, 250 practicing school
administrators were surveyed. They were asked the following:
"What three suggestions would you give a school administrator, a
friend, who had to engage in hostile conversations with adults?"
Their responses were sorted and grouped by topic, and then suggestions were ordered by rank. The participating school administrators
recommended 15 strategies they found most helpful.

Amazingly, all of these "modern-day" strategies are actually
age-old practices espoused by past generations. There are no

surprises. We know these truths. Most of us learned these strategies at the knee of a parent or grandparent in the form of adages, proverbs, or aphorisms. Success when dealing with oral confrontations appears proportionate to one's ability to apply these long-known strategies to the new situations we face today. What we must learn is how to apply them to tense verbal exchanges (Kosmoski, 1999b). Consider and apply these top 15 strategies when engaged in hostile conversations.

- Gather pertinent information. When dealing with hostile adults, it is most advantageous to have solid, accurate information about the circumstances prior to the encounter. Wise bosses foster a district climate in which administrators share information regarding potentially volatile or hostile situations. Staff members are encouraged to report any suspicion of trouble. Candor is praised. Forewarned, administrators have the time to gather pertinent information and verify facts. Effective administrators would rather prepare for 10 hostile conversations that do not materialize than be unprepared for one that does.

Forewarned is forearmed.
Cervantes

Knowledge is power.
Francis Bacon

- Defer action. One of the best techniques for resolving problems is to defer action until all parties are calm. Little is accomplished when an individual is agitated or out of control. Postpone confrontational conversations until you understand all the circumstances and the hostile adult has had time to calm down and rethink his or her position. Tell the person that you understand that his or her concern is serious and genuine. Acknowledge that you are upset and you need time to calm down. Explain to the furious individual that you need to move the meeting to a later date so there will be ample time to address his or her concerns. Do not equate delaying tactics with avoidance. Your purpose is not to run from trouble, but rather to solve a problem or dispute. Ample time is necessary to reach a satisfactory resolution (Nierenberg, 1981). Given time to temper hostile emotions, the angry individual will be more rational and generally more amenable to your point of view.

> *Fools rush in where angels fear to tread.*
> Alexander Pope

> *Timing is everything.*
> George Bums

• Refuse to be baited. It is unnecessary to verbally attack or retaliate when engaged in conversation. It is more difficult for an individual to threaten, curse, yell, or scream if the opposition chooses not to exhibit like behaviors. Usually, after an initial onslaught, the furious individual begins to calm down if you do not fuel the anger. A calm, controlled demeanor during verbal attacks is a powerful tool. Courtesy is rewarded (Cartwright & Schwartz, 1987). Remember, you are a professional who sets the tone.

> *It takes two to make a fight.*
> Unknown

> *Fools bite one another, but wise men agree together.*
> George Herbert

> *Wisdom has taught us to be calm and meek,*
> *to take one blow and turn the other cheek.*
> Oliver W. Holmes

• Compile a response list. School leaders who successfully defuse volatile conversations mentally compile a list of positive responses to use during uncomfortable discussions. These statements are designed to express concern, sincerity, reasonableness, and empathy. Examples of such responses include "I can understand your concern," "We need to . . . ," "I appreciate your effort," and "How can I help?" Take a few minutes to formulate your own personal list of calming responses. Select those that are most appropriate for you. Over time, you may add or delete individual phrases from your memory bank. Review your mental list periodically so that the responses become more familiar and comfortable to you.

Then, when a tense situation occurs, you will be prepared with responses that are natural to you and have the effect you wish.

Honey catches more flies than vinegar.
Franklin Praimanac

• Learn to apologize. When a conversation confirms that a constituent has been genuinely wronged, you must learn to apologize. This is not always an easy task. Many of us were taught that admitting fault is a sign of weakness. Not true. Sincere contrition should be perceived to be a strength rather than a weakness (Tannen, 1995). Our colleagues also suggest that using the phrase "I'm sorry" has a positive effect on those who are verbally attacking us. Even if you have no reason or intent to apologize, you can use the phrase "I'm sorry" to your advantage. Expressing regret that an angry adult feels the way he or she does has a calming effect. Try, "I'm sorry you feel this way" or "I'm sorry you have to do this." These statements do not compromise your position and yet they express comfort and empathy. One caution: Others often detect insincere apologies and view them as demeaning and manipulative.

It takes a big person to say, "I'm sorry."
Unknown

The man who is sorry over the fact will win.
Lao Tzu

We must be heartily sorry for misdoings.
St. Matthew

• Listen to body messages. Be aware of what your body tells you. During heated conversations, do not ignore or disdain butterflies in the stomach, an increase in heart rate, and other mild signs of stress. Savvy administrators view these physical changes as an advance warning system of possible danger. Heed your body and remain alert.

Fear is a good copilot.
M. Scott Carpenter, Astronaut

Fear is the beginning of wisdom.
Unknown

- Develop a plan to get help. Before any potentially dangerous incidents occur, develop a plan for seeking help. Prudent administrators prepare for true emergencies. Volatile conversations can escalate into physical encounters. Widely disseminate and implement a clear procedure for summoning help. Hesitation can have devastating consequences. Predetermined signs, gestures, or phrases should be cues for action. Here is one example. When danger seems more a probability than a possibility, an administrator might buzz the secretary to cancel an appointment with Mr. Raven. In this case, the word *Raven* serves as the trigger, or cue word, for the secretary to call authorities. Develop a plan that includes procedures, methods, individual responsibilities, and assignments. Resolve issues of chain of command, locations, and alternatives. Agree upon each procedure in detail. Provide in-service training on this topic for your entire staff. Give each responsible adult a paper copy of his or her duties.

> *An ounce of prevention is worth a pound of cure.*
> Scammell

> *To be prepared for war is one of the most*
> *effectual means of preserving peace.*
> George Washington

- Get a grip. Good administrators first control themselves before ever trying to control the situation. This is not an easy task. When we feel anger, frustration, disgust, or fear, our bodies react and make it difficult to think and act professionally. If we use the techniques for reducing stress, our bodies and, therefore, our minds will be less affected. Try the proven remedies of deep breathing, relaxing tense muscles, counting to 10, and active listening.

> *Think before you speak.*
> William Shakespeare

- Be selective when speaking. There are times when we are privy to much more information than the person who confronts us. Our peers advise that we share only pertinent and germane facts with him or her. They caution us to avoid blurting out unnecessary and peripheral facts and details. Providing the hostile individual with additional or unrelated information might confuse the issue and make defusing the situation more difficult. Also, giving the person additional facts might increase or fuel his or her negative emotions. Educators too often believe that it is our "duty" to impart knowledge. This is a misconception. We do not have to mention everything we know. By contrast, there are those occasions where supplying additional and appropriate information clarifies matters and helps resolve the conflict. Effective administrators must be thoughtful and use good judgment when sharing information.

> *Don't open a can of worms.*
> Unknown

> *If you open Pandora's Box, you never know what Trojan horses will appear.*
> Ernest Bevin

• Recognize enemies and dissenters. All of us have been faced with individuals who, for whatever reason, wish to damage our image, credibility, or reputation. They twist the meaning of our words or invent their own meanings. They embellish or exaggerate the truth. They spew venomous remarks every time our names are mentioned. These people are often the school gossips or naysayers. If we recognize them for what they are and how they can hurt us, we can defend ourselves. Avoiding conversations with such persons is a prudent practice. There is no law that requires us to talk to these people. Why waste our time? Why help them malign us?

> *Fool me once, shame on you; fool me twice, shame on me.*
> Unknown

> *Fools grow without watering.*
> Thomas Fuller

• Speak softly. Our colleagues literally suggest that we speak softly when engaged in hostile conversations. They advise us to use a low, calm voice during heated or tense verbal exchanges. Peers suggest that we make clear, reasonable, and concise statements during unpleasant confrontations. The content of our words, then, becomes our "big stick." How we say something is often as important as what we say. Volume, voice, and content must be our strengths when dealing with hostile adults.

> *Speak softly and carry a big stick.*
> Teddy Roosevelt

- Develop listening skills. Active listening skills aid us in hostile conversations. Paraphrasing and reiteration affirm understanding. Responses beginning with "Do you mean," "Let me see if I understand," and "Are you saying," are excellent verbal tools. Pointed, nonaccusing questions dispel confusion and clarify misunderstandings. Examples of useful questions are, "What exactly did you see?" "Can you give me more details?" and "What was the sequence of events?" Affirmative nodding and gentle interjections such as, "oh," "yes," and "ah" can give your opposition the courage to continue and suggest your interest and concern.

> *Listen, not just hear.*
> Unknown

> *Attention, attention must be paid to others.*
> Arthur Miller

- Utilize credible witnesses. If you have reason to expect an unpleasant meeting or heated discussion, bring one or several witnesses. The presence of others often acts as its own deterrent. In many cases, an agitated or angry individual will voluntarily monitor and temper his or her behavior if there are observers. Witnesses also act as a safeguard when a question or interpretation of an event is necessary after the confrontation.

> *Two are better than one.*
> Ecclesiastes 4:9

> *Oh, to have the strength of twenty men.*
> William Shakespeare

> *There is strength in numbers.*
> Unknown

- Remain detached. Do not personalize an attack. When individuals vent, whine, or rave, it usually has little to do with you personally. Rather, these behaviors are an expression of their own inabilities. They are frustrated, angry, and unempowered. They do not view *you* as the leader, friend, parent, or spouse. In heated exchanges, the aggressor usually thinks of you, the school administrator, as the authority figure.

> *Sticks and stones may break my bones,*
> *but names will never hurt me.*
> Mother Goose

- Move on. There are times when we must admit we did not handle a hostile conversation well. We might have been more effective in defusing a situation. After the fact, the best one can do is learn from the mistakes and move on. Excessive rumination and personal chastisement are unproductive. Get on with the business at hand and do it better the next time.

> *Don't cry over spilt milk.*
> Andrew Yamanton

> *Don't spit in the wind.*
> Jim Croce

> *Don't let your heart rule your head.*
> Unknown

Each of the above suggestions is important and worth recalling during times when we are engaged in heated or unpleasant conversations. But how can you remember so much and, at the same time, hold up your end of a discussion? Easy. Just recall those old adages learned when you were young and impressionable. The sayings will "stick" in your mind with little effort and serve as the trigger to fill in the details. Here, again, are the adages. These strategies have been grouped into two identifiable categories—perception and communication. One simple memory technique is to put each on an index card and study it. They are:

Perception:

1. Forewarned is forearmed. No surprise is a good surprise.
2. It takes two to make a fight.
3. Fear is a good copilot.
4. An ounce of prevention is worth a pound of cure.
5. Fool me once, shame on you; fool me twice, shame on me.
6. There is strength in numbers.
7. Sticks and stones may break my bones, but names will never hurt me.
8. Don't cry over spilt milk.

Communication:

9. Timing is everything. Fools rush in where angels fear to tread.
10. Honey catches more flies than vinegar.
11. It takes a big person to say, "I'm sorry."
12. Think before you speak.
13. Don't open a can of worms.
14. Speak softly and carry a big stick.
15. Listen, not just hear.

Skill in communicating is essential in our profession. Learn from other practitioners. Heed the advice of your peers. These 15 strategies are powerful tools to be utilized during hostile conversations with adults at school. The wisdom of the past can serve your present needs. If you can successfully apply these strategies during hostile conversations, you will become a more effective educational leader as you enter the new millennium.

AUTHOR'S NOTE: Unsourced quotations can be attributed to the following:

Bartlett, J. (1980). *Familiar quotations: A collection of passages, and proverbs traced to their sources in ancient and modern literature.* Boston: Little, Brown.

Chambers, A. (Ed.). (1997). *Chambers dictionary of quotations.* New York: Chambers.

Macmillan dictionary of quotations. (1989). New York: Macmillan.

Meider, W., Kingsbury, S. A., & Harder, K. (1992). *A dictionary of American proverbs.* New York: Oxford University Press.

Oxford dictionary of quotations. (1979). New York: Oxford University Press.

Sherrin, N. (Ed.). (1995). *The Oxford dictionary of humorous quotations.* New York: Oxford University Press.

Simpson, J. (Ed.). (1997). *Simpson's contemporary quotations: The most notable quotes from 1950 to the present.* New York: Harper Collins.

Resource

The School Administrators' Code of Ethics

Ten Practices by Which to Live Your Professional Life, developed by G. Kosmoski and D. Pollack

1. The School Administrator Is an Educational Leader

   Characteristics of the EDUCATIONAL leader:

   > Consistently demonstrates the personal virtues of honesty, forthrightness, fairness, loyalty, compassion, kindness, thoughtfulness, bravery, humility, appropriateness, politeness, and trustworthiness

   > Consistently demonstrates the professional qualities of vision, knowledge, trust building, decisiveness, motivation, consistency, creativity, focus, open-mindedness, flexibility, stamina, positivity, proficiency in managerial tasks, and a sense of humor

2. The School Administrator Is Committed to Education

   Characteristics of the COMMITTED administrator:

   > Works to maintain and improve the educational program

   > Focuses on the needs of the students

   > Puts the education of students before any other consideration

   > Places educational priorities before personal needs and agendas

   > Is student centered

3. The School Administrator Is Knowledgeable

Characteristics of the KNOWLEDGEABLE administrator:

Has the proper education and licensing

Regularly takes classes or attends workshops to remain current

Reads constantly—educational books, journals, reports, legal updates, etc.

Participates in professional organizations, conferences, and seminars

Keeps apprised of local, state, and national events and trends

Freely shares information and knowledge with constituents

4. The School Administrator Is Visionary

Characteristics of the VISIONARY administrator:

Sees the big picture

Promotes the good for the many

Projects future trends

Identifies quality/long-lasting solutions

Prioritizes goals and activities

5. The School Administrator Empowers Others

Characteristics of the EMPOWERING administrator:

Encourages teachers to participate in decision making

Encourages teachers to take positions of internal and external leadership

Promotes student personal and group responsibility

Promotes student ownership in his or her own education

Provides opportunities for parental and community involvement in school decisions and directions

Acknowledges and praises staff and student accomplishments

6. The School Administrator Is Trustworthy

Characteristics of the TRUSTWORTHY administrator:

Follows through on promises in a timely manner

Keeps confidences

Does not crumble under pressure

Says and does what she or he means

Remains loyal in difficult circumstances

7. The School Administrator Demands High, Achievable Expectations

Characteristics of the HIGH EXPECTATION administrator:

Sets high expectations and standards for himself or herself

Believes that all students can learn and excel

Believes in the professionalism of the staff and demands their best

Expects unequivocal support and effort from the school community

Demands good attendance from all

8. The School Administrator Is a Skilled Communicator

Characteristics of the COMMUNICATING administrator:

Disseminates regular newsletter, memo, brag sheets, and information updates

Disseminates regular parent/community newsletters

Successfully uses technology such as parent/student telephone hotlines, weekend voice mail, radio/television news spots, local newspapers, select voice- and e-mail updates, congratulation messages, and so forth

Takes time to visit and chat with all constituents including the school board members, community service CEO's, neighbors, parents, teachers, and support staff

9. The School Administrator Is Available

Characteristics of the AVAILABLE administrator:

Engages in management by walking (MBW)—is found daily in the school classrooms, hallways, meeting areas, conference rooms, lounges, etc.

Returns calls promptly

Establishes open office hours

Attends school functions and extracurricular activities

10. The School Administrator Is Visible in the Community

Characteristics of the VISIBLE administrator:

Participates in civic functions

Joins and attends civic organizations

Represents the school community at local, regional, and state political meetings, etc.

Note: This study was conducted at Governors State University in University Park, Illinois by the authors. In 1997, an initial 200 participators—100 aspiring school administrators, 50 veteran administrators, and 50 teachers—from various settings and locations were asked to list the behaviors and practices of the ideal school administrator. In 2004, the study was expanded to include an additional 100 participants nationwide—50 practitioners and 50 aspiring. The above code reflects a compilation and synthesis of these 300 responses.

References

Acheson, K. A., & Gall, M. D. (1992). *Techniques in the clinical supervision of teachers* (3rd ed.). White Plains, NY: Longman.

Ambrosio, J. (2004). No Child Left Behind: The case of Roosevelt High School. *Phi Delta Kappan, 85*(9), 709–712.

American Association of School Administrators Executive Board. (1976). *The code of ethics for school administrators.* Retrieved June 2004 from www.aasa.org

American Psychiatric Association. (1994). *Diagnostic and statistical manual of mental disorders* (4th ed.). Washington, DC: Author.

American Psychological Association. (2004). *Obeying and resisting malevolent orders.* Retrieved June 19, 2004 from www.apa.org

Anderson, M., MacDonald, D. S., & Sinnemann, C. (2004). Can measurement of results help improve the performance of schools? *Phi Delta Kappan, 85*(10), 735–739.

Armistead, L. (1996, April). What to do before the violence happens: Designing the crisis communication plan. *NASSP Bulletin, 77*(552), 31–37.

Association of Supervision and Curriculum Development. (2004, Spring). *An insider's view of ASCD: Taking understanding by design to the next level* (pp. 1–3). Arlington, VA: ASCD Associate News.

Bailey, J. (1990). *The serenity principle.* San Francisco: Harper & Row.

Bandura, A. (1977). *Social learning theory.* Englewood Cliffs, NJ: Prentice Hall.

Barr, R., & Tagg, J. (1995, November–December). From teaching to learning. *Change, 27*(6), 13–25.

Bartlett, J. (1980). *Familiar quotations: A collection of passages, and proverbs traced to their sources in ancient and modern literature.* Boston: Little, Brown.

Berman, S. (1998). The bridge to civility: Empathy, ethics, and service. *School Administrator, 55*(4), 52–58.

Bruer, J. T. (1998). Brain science, brain fiction. *Educational Leadership, 56*(3), 14–19.

Burrello, L. C., Hoffman, L. P., & Murray, L. E. (2004). *Building capacity from within: Solving competing agendas creatively.* Thousand Oaks, CA: Corwin.

Byham, W. (with Cox, J., & Harper, K.). (1992). *Zapp! In education.* New York: Fawcett Columbine.

Cambron-McCabe, N., Cunningham, L. L., Harvey, J., & Koff, R. H. (2004). *The superintendents' fieldbook: A guide for leaders of learning.* Thousand Oaks, CA: Corwin with AASA.

Carey, B. (2004, June 22). Fear in the workplace: The bullying boss. *New York Times,* pp. D1, D6.

Carlson, R. (1997). *Don't sweat the small stuff . . . and it's all small stuff.* New York: Hyperion.

Cartwright, G., & Schwartz, A. (1987). *The school official's guide to student discipline hearings.* Springfield, IL: Illinois Association of School Boards.

Cavarretta, J. (1998). Parents are the school's best friend. *Educational Leadership, 55*(8), 12–15.

Chambers, A. (Ed.). (1997). *Chambers dictionary of quotations.* New York: Chambers.

Chambers, L. (1998). How customer-friendly is your school? *Educational Leadership, 56*(2), 33–35.

Charlesworth, E. A., & Nathan, R. G. (1985). *Stress management: A comprehensive guide to wellness.* New York: Ballantine.

Chase, B. (1998). NEA's role: Cultivating teacher professionalism. *Educational Leadership, 55*(5), 18–20.

Child, R. (1998). Children are more likely to excel in school when their parents are involved. *Jet, 46*(1), 46–47.

Cohan, E. G., & Lotan, R. A. (1995). Producing equal-status interaction in heterogeneous classrooms. *American Educational Research Journal, 32*(1), 99–120.

Collins, J. (2001). *Good to great: Why some companies make the leap . . . and others don't.* New York: Harper Collins.

Council of Chief State School Officers. (1996, November). *The Interstate School Leaders Licensure Consortium Standards for School Leaders* (ISLLC Standards). Retrieved June 2004 from www.ccsso.org

Covey, S. R. (1990). *Seven habits of highly effective people: Powerful lessons in personal change.* New York: Franklin Covey.

Cragan, J. F., & Wright, D. W. (1995). *Communications in small groups: Theory, process, skills* (4th ed.). St. Paul, MN: West.

Davison, M., Young, S. S., Davenport, E., Butterbaugh, D., & Davison, L. (2004). Why do children fall behind? What can be done? *Phi Delta Kappan, 85*(10), 752–761.

Dixon, R. (1994). Future schools and how to get there from here. *Phi Delta Kappan, 75*(3), 360–365.

Estep, S. G. (2003). Community relations. In Kaiser, J. (Ed.), *Educational administration* (3rd ed., pp. 110–112). Mequon, WI: Stylex Press.

Felder, L. (1994, October 15). How to deal with difficult people at work. *Bottom Line/Personal*, p. 1.

Finn, J. (1998). Parent engagement that makes a difference. *Educational Leadership, 55*(8), 20–24.

Freiberg, H. J. (1998). Measuring school climate: Let me count the ways. *Educational Leadership, 56*(1), 22–27.

Fried, R. (1995). *The passionate teacher.* Boston: Beacon.

Gardner, H. (1994). *The arts and human development.* New York: Basic Books.

Gardner, H. (1995). *Leading minds: An anatomy of leadership.* New York: Basic Books.

Gatchel, R. J., & Blanchard, E. B. (1993). *Psychophysiological disorders.* Washington, DC: American Psychological Association.

Gates, S. M., Ringel, J. S., Santibanez, L., Chung, C. H., & Ross, K. (2003). *Who is leading our schools? An overview of school administrators and their careers.* New York: Rand.

Gersten, R., Fuchs, L. S., Williams, J. P., & Baker, S. (2001). Teaching reading comprehension strategies to students with learning disabilities: A review of research. *Review of Educational Research, 71*(2), 279–320.

Gladwell, M. (1998, August). Do parents matter? *New Yorker, 74*(24), 55–65.

Glanz, J., & Neville, R. F. (1997). *Educational supervision: Perspectives, issues, and controversies.* Norwood, MA: Christopher-Gordon.

Glasser, W. (1997). A new look at school failure and school success. *Phi Delta Kappan, 78*(8), 596–602.

Glickman, C. D. (1990). *Supervision of instruction: A developmental approach* (2nd ed.). Boston: Allyn & Bacon.

Glomb, T. M. (2002). Workplace anger and aggression. Informing conceptual models with data from specific encounters. *Journal of Occupational Health Psychology, 7*(1), 20–36.

Goleman, D. (1998). *Emotional intelligence.* New York: Bantam.

Goleman, D., Boyatzes, R., & McKee, A. (2002). *Primal leadership: Realizing the power of emotional intelligence.* Boston: Harvard Business Press.

Gordon, R. (1998). Balancing real-world problems with real-world results. *Phi Delta Kappan, 79*(4), 390–394.

Gulick, L., & Urwick, L. (1937). *Papers on the science of administration.* New York: Institute of Public Administration, Columbia University.

Hackman, J. R., & Oldham, G. R. (1976). Motivation through the design of work. *Organizational Behavior & Human Decision Processes, 16*(2), 250–279.

Hansen, M., & Childs, J. (1998). Creating a school where people like to be. *Educational Leadership, 56*(1), 14–17.

Hodges, D. (2004). *Looking forward to Monday morning: Ideas for recognition and appreciation activities and fun things to do at work for educators.* Thousand Oaks, CA: Corwin.

Hoyle, J. R., Bjork, L. G., Collier, V., & Glass, T. (2004). *The superintendent as CEO: Standard-based performance.* Thousand Oaks, CA: Corwin with AASA.

Illinois Federation of Teachers. (1999). What parents want from their children's schools: Strong academic standards seen as most important. *Union News, 4*(3), 6–7.

Jacobson, E. (1938). *Progressive relaxation* (2nd ed.). Chicago: University of Chicago Press.

Johnson, D. W., & Johnson, R. T. (1991). *Teaching students to be peacemakers.* Edina, MN: Interaction.

Johnson, D. W., & Johnson, R. T. (1997). Conflict resolution and peer mediation in elementary and secondary schools: A review of the research. *Review of Educational Research, 66*(4), 459–506.

Kaiser, J. S. (2003). *Educational Administration* (3rd ed.). Mequon, WI: Stylex Press.

Karasek, R. A. (1979). Job demands, job decision latitude, and mental strain: Implications for job redesign. *Administrative Science Quarterly, 24,* 285–308.

Kelly, P. A., Brown, S., Butler, A., Pelah, G., Taylor, C., & Zeller, P. (1998). A place to hang our hats. *Educational Leadership, 56*(1), 62–64.

Kersting, K. (2004). Stepping in when schools fail. *American Psychological Association Monitor, 35*(3), 36.

Kierkegaard, S. (1980). *The concept of anxiety.* Princeton, NJ: Princeton University Press.

Kohn, A. (1996). *Beyond discipline: From compliance to community.* Alexandria, VA: Association for Supervision and Curriculum Development.

Kosmoski, G. J. (1999a). Defusing a conversation that turns hostile. *The School Administrator, 3*(56), 35.

Kosmoski, G. J. (1999b). *How to land the best jobs in school administration* (Rev ed.). Thousand Oaks, CA: Corwin.

Kosmoski, G. J. (2001). *Supervision* (2nd ed.). Mequon, WI: Stylex.

Kosmoski, G. J., & Pollack, D. R. (1997, February). *Effects of a mentor program for beginning school administrators.* Paper presented at the National Conference of the Eastern Educational Research Association, Hilton Head, SC.

Kosmoski, G. J., & Pollack, D. R. (Speakers). (1998, February/March). *From Jekyll to Hyde: The changes of beginning school administrators* (Cassette Recording No. AASA98–80). American Association of School Administrators 130th National Conference on Education, San Diego, CA.

Kosmoski, G. J., & Pollack, D. R. (1999). *Talking with hostile adults at school.* Paper presented at the National Conference on Education, American Association of School Administrators, New Orleans, LA.

Kosmoski, G. J., Pollack, D. R., & Schmidt, L. J. (1999). Jekyll or Hyde: Changes in leadership styles and the personalities of beginning school administrators. *Illinois Schools Journal, 79*(1), 23–34.

Kottler, J. A. (1997). *Success with challenging students.* Thousand Oaks, CA: Corwin.

LaBrecque, R. (1998). *Effective department and team leaders.* Norwood, MA: Christopher-Gordon.

Lambert, L. (1998). How to build leadership capacity. *Educational Leadership, 55*(7), 17–19.

Lasley, T. J. (1998). Paradigm shifts in the classroom. *Phi Delta Kappan, 80*(1), 84–86.

Lazear, D. (1991). *Seven ways of knowing: Teaching for multiple intelligences* (2nd ed.). Palatine, IL: IRI/Skylight.

Lee, J. (with Stott, B.). (1993). *Facing the fire: Experiencing and expressing anger appropriately.* New York: Bantam.

Levinas, E. (1995). *Ethics and infinity.* Pittsburgh, PA: Duquesne University Press.

Lewis, C. A. (1998). Seeking connections through character. *Phi Delta Kappan, 80*(2), 99–100.

Lewis, M. L., & Carifio, J. (1997). Ratings of assault vignettes. *Journal of Research in Education, 7*(1), 40–47.

Mackie, J. L. (1990). *Ethics: Inventing right and wrong.* New York: Penguin.

Macmillan dictionary of quotations. (1989). New York: Macmillan.

Martin, J. R. (1995). A philosophy of education for the year 2000. *Phi Delta Kappan, 76*(5), 355–359.

Martinez, M. C. (2004). *Teachers working together for school success.* Thousand Oaks, CA: Corwin.

Mastropieri, M., & Scruggs, T. E. (1997). Best practices in promoting reading comprehension in students with learning disabilities: 1976 to 1996. *Remedial and Special Education, 18*(4), 197–213.

McEwan, E. K. (2004). *How to deal with parents who are angry, afraid, or just plain crazy* (2nd ed.). Thousand Oaks, CA: Corwin.

Meider, W., Kingsbury, S. A., & Harder, K. (1992). *A dictionary of American proverbs.* New York: Oxford University Press.

Michigan Department of Education. (2000). *School violence.* Retrieved May 2004 from www.michigan.gov/hal/0,1607,7-160-18835_18897-52905—,oo.html

Moriarity, A., Maeyama, R. G., & Fitzgerald, P. J. (1993). A clear plan for school crisis management. *NASSP Bulletin, 77*(552), 17–22.

Morrison, A. M., White, R. P., & Van Velsor, E. (1987, August). Executive women: Substance plus style. *Psychology Today, 21*(8), 18–26.

Nelson, W. W. (1998). The naked truth about school reform in Minnesota. *Phi Delta Kappan, 79*(9), 679–684.

Nierenberg, G. I. (1981). *The art of negotiating.* New York: Simon & Schuster.

Oglesby, C. (2001). *Teachers: Low pay, low morale, high turnover.* Retrieved May 2004 from http://cnnstudentnews.cnn.com/SPECIALS/2001/schools/stories/staff.effects.html

Oliva, P. F. (1993). *Supervision for today's schools* (2nd ed.). White Plains, NY: Longman.

Olson, C. (1998). Parent involvement in middle level activities. *Educational Leadership, 55*(8), 34–35.

Oxford dictionary of quotations. (1979). New York: Oxford University Press.

Panico, A. P. (1999). *Discipline & the classroom community: Recapturing control of our schools.* Mequon, WI: Stylex.

Pellicer, L. O. (2004). *Caring enough to lead: How reflective thought leads to moral leadership* (2nd ed.). Thousand Oaks, CA: Corwin.

Peterson, K. D., & Deal, T. E. (1998). How leaders influence the culture of schools. *Educational Leadership, 56*(1), 28–31.

Phillips, P. (1997). The conflict wall. *Educational Leadership, 54*(8), 43–44.

Piper, D. L. (1974). Decisionmaking: Decisions made by individuals vs. those made by group consensus or group participation. *Educational Administration Quarterly, 10*(2), 82–95.

Pryor, P. W., & Pryor, C. R. (2004). *The school leaders' guide to understanding attitude and influencing behavior: Working with teachers, parents, students, and the community.* Thousand Oaks, CA: Corwin.

Queen, J. A. (2004). *The frazzled principal's wellness plan: Reclaiming time, managing stress, and creating a healthy lifestyle.* Thousand Oaks, CA: Corwin.

Ramsey, R. D. (2004). *What matters most for school leaders: 25 reminders of what is really important.* Thousand Oaks, CA: Corwin.

Render, G. F., Padilla, J. M., & Krank, H. M. (1989). Assertive discipline: A critical review and analysis. *Teachers College Record, 90*(5), 607–630.

Riley, R. (1996). Invite America back to your school this year. *Principal, 76*(1), 30.

Rose, L. C., & Gallup, A. M. (2003). The 35th annual Phi Delta Kappa/Gallup poll of the public's attitudes toward the public schools. *Phi Delta Kappan, 85*(1), 38–56.

Rubin, J. (1998). Training knows no bounds. *NEA Today, 15*(3), 334–336.

Ryan, K., & Bohlin, K. E. (1999). *Building character in schools.* San Francisco: Jossey-Bass.

Schmidt, L. (1997). *Schools and society.* University Park, IL: Governors State University Press.

Schwartz, T. (1995). *What really matters?* New York: Bantam.

Sergiovanni, T. J., & Starratt, R. J. (1988). *Supervision: Human perspectives* (4th ed.). New York: McGraw-Hill.

Shanker, A. (1995, Spring). Classrooms held hostage: The disruption of the many by the few. *American Federation of Teachers*, 10–13, 47.

Sherrin, N. (Ed.). (1995). *The Oxford dictionary of humorous quotations*. New York: Oxford University Press.

Simonelli, R. (1996, Winter). The basic school: Recreating community for educational development. *Winds of Change, 11*(1), 22–25.

Simpson, J. (Ed.). (1997). *Simpson's contemporary quotations: The most notable quotes from 1950 to the present*. New York: Harper Collins.

Simpson, M. D. (1998). Taking threats seriously. *NEA Today, 17*, 27.

Skinner, B. F. (1953). *Science in human behavior.* New York: Macmillan.

Spring, J. (1991). *American education: An introduction to social and political aspects* (5th ed.). White Plains, NY: Longman.

SuiChu, E., & Willm, J. (1996). Effects of parent involvement on eighth grade achievement. *Sociology of Education, 69*(2), 126–141.

State of California. (2001, May). *The California Professional Standards for Educational Leaders* (CPSELS). Retrieved July 2004 from www.acsa.org/doc_files/CPSELS%20card.pdf

Stone, S., Patton, B., Heen, S., & Fisher, R. (2000). *Difficult conversations: How to discuss what matters most*. New York: Penguin.

Suinn, R. M. (2001). The terrible twos: Anger and anxiety hazardous to your health. *American Psychology, 56*(1), 27–36.

Tannen, D. (1995). *Talking from 9 to 5: Women and men in the workplace: Language, sex and power.* New York: Avon.

Toby, J. (1993–1994, Winter). Everyday school violence: How disorder fuels it. *American Educator, 17*(1), 4–9, 44–48.

Uchida, D., Cetron, M., & McKenzie, F. (1996). What students must know to succeed in the 21st century. *The Futurist, 30*(4), 7.

U.S. Department of Education. (2004a). *Crime and safety in America's public schools: Selected findings from the school survey on crime and safety.* Retrieved July 2004 from http://nces.ed.gov/pubsearch/pub sinfo.asp?pubid=2004370

U.S. Department of Education. (2004b). *Indicators of school crime and safety: 2003.* Retrieved July 2004 from http://nces.ed.gov/pubsearch/pubsinfo.asp?pubid=2004004

Wasserstein, A. G., Shea, J. A., Mulhern, V., & Field, M. (2003). *Faculty work climate survey: 2003.* Retrieved June 2004 from www.med.upenn.edu/facaffrs/fpd/documents/Facultyclimatesurvey12.ppt

Williams, B. (1985). *Ethics and the limits of philosophy.* Cambridge, MA: Harvard University Press.

Williamson, M. (1997). *The healing of America.* New York: Simon & Schuster.

Wilson, I. (1995, January 13). Prepare to take effective control. *New York Times Educational Supplement*, A6.

Index